The construction follows the pattern of a landscape, with the auditorium seen as a valley, and there at its bottom is the orchestra surrounded by a sprawling vineyard climbing the sides of its neighbouring hills. The ceiling, resembling a tent, encounters this "landscape" like a "skyscape." Convex in character, the tent-like ceiling is very much linked with the acoustics, with the desire to obtain the maximum diffusion of music via the convex surfaces. Here the sound is not reflected from the narrow side of a hall, but rises from the depth and centre, moving towards all sides, then descending and spreading evenly among the listeners below. Every effort was taken to transmit the sound waves to the most distant part of the auditorium by the shortest possible route. The diffusion is also served by the reflection of the auditorium walls, and the multi-leveled, heterogeneous arrangement of the "vineyard terraces." In all this we were greatly aided by progress made in the field of acoustic science: virgin territory was discovered, explored and conquered. The demands of the auditorium determine every last constructional detail of this monumental building. Even as far as the exterior form is concerned, a fact so clearly demonstrated by the tent-like shape of the roof. The construction of the auditorium — built as it is over the main foyer — also determined the character of the ancillary space. Every room had ample opportunity for the free development of its own particular function. Even the complex of stairways seems to play about the foyer, yet rhythmically adapting its lively form to the demands of the auditorium. Thus, all is directed towards the preparation of the heightened experience. The ancillary space stands in a dynamic and tense relationship to the festive calm of the auditorium, which is truly the jewel in the philharmonic crown. HANS S

G000131392

PHILIPPA GAMMIE

DEVELOPED AND DESIGNED BY studio bau:ton AND whitenoise

SOUNDSPACE

ARCHITECTURE FOR SOUND AND VISION

PETER GRUENEISEN

BIRKHÄUSER — PUBLISHERS FOR ARCHITECTURE

BASEL · BOSTON · BERLIN

CONTENT

SOUNDSPACE ARCHITECTURE FOR SOUND AND VISION

Architektur ist überhaupt
die erstarrte Musik.

FRIEDRICH VON SCHELLING

La vue d'un tel monument est comme
une musique continuelle et fixée.

ANNE LOUISE GERMAINE DE STAËL-HOLSTEIN

I call architecture frozen music.

JOHANN WOLFGANG VON GOETHE

Can architecture be heard? Most people would probably say that as architecture does not produce sound, it cannot be heard. But neither does it radiate light and yet it can be seen. We see the light it reflects and thereby gain an impression of form and material. In the same way we hear the sounds it reflects and they, too, give us an impression of form and material. Differently shaped rooms and different materials reverberate differently. STEEN EILER RASMUSSEN

INTRODUCTION

ARCHITECTURE FOR SOUND AND VISION

ARCHITECTURE AND MUSIC

Architecture is frozen music. Music is thawed architecture. Are simple and familiar statements like these doing justice to the complexity of the subject? How can the two arts be compared or juxtaposed? Or, just as importantly, how can they coexist and interact with each other when they come together and intersect? That is the central theme of this book, although the definition of music has been conveniently expanded here to include movies and other contemporary media.

Parallels between buildings and sound have been recognized and contemplated for centuries, maybe since the very beginning of discourse about either. Intersecting elements and common threads can be found in the conceptual and theoretical realm, where structural similarities between music and architecture are frequently explored during creative conception, or later identified and analyzed in retrospect. Architects have always referred to buildings in terms borrowed from the musical vocabulary, while musicians have studied the architecture and structure of compositions. Connections and analogies can be made convincingly between individual buildings and musical pieces, or between entire movements and styles in architectural and musical history. Comparing the two disciplines is one of the most commonplace and stereotypical endeavors, and yet it can still generate exciting results and insights, often in unexpected ways.

On a subjective level, expressions and feelings can often be intuitively understood to connect, or separate, a piece of music and a particular building. The Experience Music Project by Frank Gehry in Seattle seems to evoke the spirit of Jimi Hendrix, its initial inspiration, and rock music in general, on a visceral level. Other buildings, for example the Rock 'n' Roll Hall of Fame in Cleveland, can fail to live up to their stated goal of representing rock music and conjuring up its spirit. Examples like this can be found for every type and style of music. It seems that without an intuitive understanding of the creative substance of both disciplines, neither theoretical nor historical knowledge is sufficient to grasp the emotional potential of the music or the building. Countless other structures exist where a musical connection can be made instinctively, or where an attempt has been made to link the two by design, successfully or not.

An even closer relationship between architecture and music emerges when buildings have the express purpose of accommodating music and sounds. Concert halls, buildings with a sharp focus on acoustic parameters, are prime examples of a very clear and obvious connection. Here, the relationship between the musical performance and the architectural environment exists on a very practical and programmatic level. The immense variety of potential architectural expressions for similar programs affords much personal interpretation and translation of the given design task. And shifting approaches over time reflect the changing attitude and perception of both the sounds and the buildings. The same goes for many other kinds of building designed for sound performances of all kinds, or for the visual and performing arts in general: opera houses and movie theaters, concert arenas and dance halls, jazz clubs and bandstands – the list goes on.

BUILDINGS FOR MEDIA PRODUCTION

Building types that are even more specifically in the service of audio and visual media have recently begun to make their appearance. While many of these buildings are concealed from public view and consciousness, they nonetheless play a large role in support of the public consumption of entertainment media, which is now omnipresent. Driven by ongoing developments in science and technology, but also by the arts and culture in general, these buildings and facilities are continually evolving.

In many ways these projects are the opposite of the open and public venues for the live enjoyment of culture with which most people are familiar. Without being widely accessible and visible to the general public, they are the workplaces and creative environments for a relatively small group of specialized insiders. The vast infrastructure of facilities, equipment and services required to produce contemporary music albums, movies and television shows goes largely unnoticed. But as secluded as they may be, these places can offer glimpses of insight into the larger issues at stake.

Despite their low public visibility, media production facilities have many features in common with public performance spaces. In a concentrated and focused manner, the requirements of today's entertainment media come together all at once. These projects demand solutions that truly bridge architecture, art and technology.

There certainly are many technical and constructive issues to be pointed out for this type of building. The central theme, however, is the relationship between the actual buildings and the reason they exist in the first place: without the songs, the music, or the movies, there would be no point in erecting any of these structures.

01 Helsinki Music Center, Competition, Computer Study, Helsinki
02–03 Extasy Records Entrance, Hollywood
04 Helmet, causing rotation of visual perception, SCI-Arc, Los Angeles

02–03

Projects of this kind, dedicated to the creative output of musicians, filmmakers and others, have constituted a large portion of our architectural work. During the process of evaluating programs, laying out plans and sections, choosing materials, and deciding on the architectural expression of a project, more elusive questions about the meaning and significance of the work come to mind.

We are interested in how spaces used in the making of sound and vision should be designed. We believe that they are not merely technical tools in the service of an unrelated art form for a different and distinct purpose. It is obvious to us that their existence in itself informs and contributes to the results obtained within. And we think that a holistic approach, one that includes an understanding of the culture and philosophies of the end product, is necessary to conceive a successful design. We are convinced that the basics of architectural design still apply to these structures, regardless of whether their focus is on external stimuli, such as music or films. Clarity of space and structure, the guiding of natural light, and coherence between the building's substance and appearance always remain important.

Clearly we believe that these spaces and buildings make a difference beyond their pure technical functionality. This is particularly true where physical spaces and their uses are connected so strongly. Being more than merely enclosures, these structures engage the ephemeral media on a fundamental level, and themselves start acting as instruments, shaping the results through their presence.

As much as the choice of instruments determines the sound of a song, the spaces inhabited while making the music influence the final result. Just as the methodology used in building design can affect the final built structure, the physical environment is an important factor within the creative process of making sounds and images.

ABOUT THIS BOOK

This book is an eclectic survey of issues we have encountered while designing and constructing buildings for the production and presentation of media content. These issues range widely, from the purely technological to concerns of building design and construction, from acoustics to ergonomics, to education, and ultimately to questions situated in the realms of philosophy and art.

The following collection represents a highly subjective view, centered around the work of our firm, studio bau:ton, and its affiliates over the last dozen years or so. The variety and complexity of these unique building types does not permit complete and objective documentation, and much of this book is necessarily confined to our own personal history and experience within the field.

Being practitioners, and not scholars or researchers, our expertise is rooted in daily practice, and our perspective is therefore restricted and somewhat biased. But we have nonetheless attempted to broaden our vision, and made an effort to include work and ideas that can explain and elaborate on our own limited knowledge and outlook.

ARCHITECTURE / ART / TECHNOLOGY

The encroachment of media into every aspect of modern life makes it necessary to have a thorough understanding of contemporary culture, art and technology if one wants to build facilities for the production of sound and pictures.

Movies, television, radio, music, computer and video games, and Internet content are an important and pervasive part of contemporary culture. We are not interested here in whether this media explosion is good or bad, or when enough is enough. However, as we design the infrastructure for the production of all this programming content, opportunities inevitably arise to examine its significance. The inherent difference between the solid physical existence of most building structures and the ephemeral nature of most media is worth examining.

Many of the projects shown here are directly concerned with the intersection, and sometimes collision, between physical structures and transitory media. However, a much better understanding of these issues can be gained by looking to the artists, architects and engineers who are intimately involved with different sides of the same themes. We were lucky to find, and obtain access to, such an outstanding collection of materials. We are grateful to the authors who have agreed to let us include their work. Their contributions are central to this book, and their insights help to position the rest of the material in a much broader context than we could have provided.

Brandon LaBelle's historical survey of artists working with sound and space, and his own continuing work as an artist and curator in the field, present a fascinating overview of the theoretical realm within the art world. In the article on Coop Himmelb(l)au's architecture and the Rolling Stones' music, visionary architect Wolf Prix draws parallels between these two bodies of work and gets to the root of the commonalities between them. Daniel Ott is a contemporary composer, and architect Peter Zumthor's musical collaborator on the Swiss Sound Pavilion, so his reflections are based on one of the most thoroughly comprehensive projects linking the two art forms – along with fashion design, food, and performance art. The Silophone project, described by Thomas McIntosh, is a true and powerful example of the potential synergies between architecture, art and technology. Finally, Bob Hodas explains his perspective as a sound engineer and "room tuner," and delivers a sharply focused view on the very specific task of optimizing the acoustics of an audio control room. Together, these authors from divergent backgrounds and with varying views paint a picture of a diverse and complex field of investigation. Work like theirs is an inspiration as we go about designing buildings of our own.

ACOUSTICS

Acoustics is the central scientific discipline to the subject of sound and space, and most closely associated with many of the featured essays and projects. Our teaching involvement at the Southern California Institute of Architecture in Los Angeles, and Full Sail Real World Education in Orlando has allowed us to think about a basic outline of architectural acoustics. The two schools, while generally focused on very different goals, share an overlapping interest in the subject, and it has been a very rewarding experience to compare the two. Full Sail, which provides a practice-oriented short-term training in media production, has shown us the value of providing straightforward instructions and basic explanations of fundamental concepts. For many of these students, excursions into related areas such as art and architecture have been an exciting and new experience. At SCI-Arc great academic curiosity is a normal condition, and the schedule, which includes class projects, has resulted in very diverse investigations into the conditions of architecture, sound and film by many of the students.

As a result of that involvement, and out of the need to organize and present our basic knowledge about acoustics, a portion of this book is dedicated to a summary of acoustical issues. The chapter is not meant to be exhaustive or profoundly scientific, but to serve as a guide to complement the other parts of this collection.

PROJECTS

A large portion of this book is dedicated to a portfolio of completed work by studio bau:ton since its founding in 1990. The subject of building and sound was, as the company name suggests, of great importance from the start. The combination of "bau" (building) and "ton" (sound) reflected not only the company's Swiss origins, but also the type of projects that were of interest to the founders from the beginning. The initial resemblance between "bau:ton" and "bauhaus" was not entirely unintentional either, as a reminder of some core values shared with the ground-breaking modern school and movement, and its comprehensive approach to design.

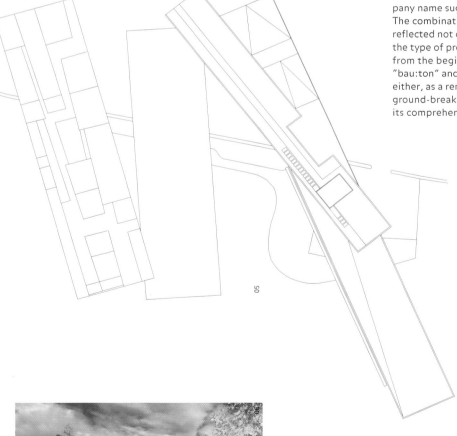

01 Palos Verdes Art Center, Competition, Palos Verdes
02–06 Tomihiro Shi-Ga Museum, Competition, Japan
07 Place for the Swiss Abroad, Competition, Brunnen, Switzerland

We hope to have created a loose symbiosis between the body of work presented here and the accompanying chapters. The illustrated projects should help to explain and illuminate the points made in other parts of the book, and vice versa. At the same time, we are excited to have this opportunity to present and expose the work of our studio to a wider audience, beyond the industries where most of the projects are centered and possibly recognized. It is our hope that some of the design solutions and answers to very specific problems will find a broader application in other realms, and for other building types.

01

SPECIALIZATION OR GENERALIZATION (OR BOTH?)

While the focus of this book is on a specific type of structure, the general approach to their design has to be understood as part of a larger view.

Over two millennia ago, Marcus Vitruvius Pollio suggested very specific design solutions for theaters and acoustic devices. His greatest emphasis however, was on the universality of architectural education and thought. In the introduction to his *Ten Books on Architecture*, he pointed to the importance of a broad and comprehensive education and attitude for architects. He demanded specialized knowledge of history, philosophy, medicine, law, astronomy and music. From this diverse background, he concluded, it is the architect's task to extract, through expertise and reasoning, whatever is appropriate for each project.

The sum of human knowledge – if not necessarily wisdom – has increased greatly since Vitruvius's time, and it keeps growing at an exponential rate. It is no longer possible for anyone to know everything within any one discipline, let alone all of them combined. But the basic premise remains true today: architecture has to be rooted in its cultural environment, and its creators must be aware of the broader context.

02

The types of project described in this book might suggest a need for narrowly specialized designers for their successful execution. Detailed knowledge of the technological apparatus in music recording studios, film editing facilities, or other media production rooms is undoubtedly necessary, but the overarching discipline required for all these projects is that of architecture as a general practice.

The simultaneous practice of residential, commercial and institutional architecture is imperative to our understanding of the broader design problems. Simply fulfilling the basic technical functions of a project will produce only mundane solutions, while including more elusive and less utilitarian aspects is a prerequisite for higher architectural quality. The technical demands of any building should always be balanced with the needs of the people who use it. The creation of a livable, exciting and outstanding physical environment remains at the core of each project, and is inherently an architectural responsibility. That most basic of architectural tasks is best honed with projects of varying types, many of them outside the scope of this book.

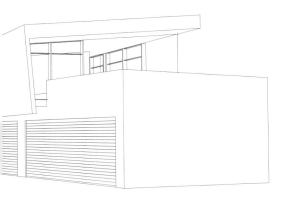

Occupying ourselves with residential design is the most straightforward way of exploring the basic needs of human habitation. We are fortunate enough to live and practice in a location that has inspired some of the most interesting and far-sighted conceptions of residential design in the twentieth century. In Los Angeles, architects like R.M. Schindler, Richard Neutra and Gregory Ain, Charles and Ray Eames, and other designers of the case-study program have reinvented the way dwellings are planned and inhabited. They, and others since, have set a great precedent for modern housing in this city. The design of the few houses we have been able to complete is not a frivolous pursuit, but a useful exercise in exploring the nature of living in and around buildings. All these benefits of course, are merely bonuses added to the great satisfaction of completing these residential projects themselves.

Another building type of great interest to us is the public cultural institution. In architectural competitions for public places and museums we can investigate how the distinctions between these projects and media facilities are becoming increasingly blurred. We perceive a narrowing of the gap between the traditional ways of presenting art and the sort of digital media produced in the facilities on which this book focuses. Art leads in the challenge to the boundaries between different kinds of media, and it is forever appropriating new technologies for originally unintended purposes. In the process, the public institutions and buildings dedicated to art are transforming themselves, becoming more interactive and multimedia oriented. In projects like the Queens Museum of Art competition, and others mentioned in these pages, we were able to explore not only the technical possibilities but also the greater significance of art and media.

Being too narrowly occupied with a single building or building type makes it easy to ignore broader issues. Recording studios and similar facilities rarely have a significant impact on urban planning and design. Their significance pales in comparison with the problems caused by housing shortages, urban blight and suburban sprawl, lack of public transportation and many other unresolved issues. As Rem Koolhaas points out, entire cities for millions of people are growing in China, Africa and elsewhere, while we are preoccupied with very small and exclusive problems of minor importance to most people. While this should in no way discourage us from making the best of these projects, it doesn't hurt to be aware of their relatively limited significance in the big picture.

Another area that deserves greater attention with regard to technologically advanced projects is that of sustainability, energy conservation and environmental sensitivity. Creating contemporary media requires large amounts of energy and resources. The general awareness of these issues is not very high within the community of engineers, producers and technicians, and is overshadowed by other concerns more directly pertinent to their work. It makes sense to use more of the sophisticated technologies now available to maximize energy efficiency in the service of buildings that are themselves highly technological. In these energy-intensive projects there is every prospect of decreasing reliance on traditional non-renewable resources by means of solar and other alternative power sources.

01–02 Residence, Bell Canyon
03–04 Residence, Hermosa Beach
05 Addition to R. Neutra's Freedman House, Pacific Palisades
06 Addition to R.M. Schindler's Elliot House, Silver Lake
07 Second Floor Addition to Residence, Mar Vista

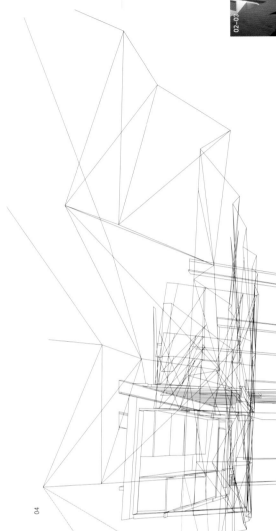

The use of sustainable and healthy building materials is another concern that should be addressed within this context. Alternatives to questionable acoustic materials such as fiberglass or lead are starting to become more widely available. With many of the traditional design and engineering issues now becoming more routine, the emphasis can shift to those questions.

As in many other areas of design, the planning of media facilities creates an interesting paradox: on the one hand, increasingly complex and specialized requirements demand intimate familiarity with the programs and processes common in the user's industries. On the other, the ability to understand the broader picture, and to see beyond the narrow confines of specific problems, has always been the most valuable service architects can provide. Ultimately, specialization can only work within the context of a comprehensive cultural understanding.

FOR AN EXPANDED PRACTICE

There is no doubt that the equipment, the technological infrastructure, the acoustics and the building systems for media production projects require special attention and in-depth consideration. Often, these aspects are handed over by architects to specialized consultants, who can handle their specific areas with ease and confidence. Indeed, every one of these projects is a team effort, depending on many people and groups with varied backgrounds and expertise. But in addition to the inclusion of specialists, we propose an expansion of the architect's own general knowledge and understanding in the interest of a comprehensive planning process.

From the start it has been our goal to narrow the gap between the disciplines, and to take back some of the responsibility that has been abandoned by architects over time. In order to deal successfully with the tasks in hand, the development of our business structures and the general approach to projects has not always followed the traditional path. We have found it necessary to blur some hallowed professional boundary lines. When we first started planning small recording studios it was clear that there were no budgets for professional acoustical engineering. It was also clear to us that we didn't want to provide the type of design commonly used in these situations, based on vague knowledge and guesswork. The resulting approach, a self-taught expansion of our basic acoustic understanding (grounded in a thorough Swiss architectural science education), and its application within architectural principles, has served us well since then. Of course we had to be aware of the limitations posed by this method, and get help and support when we needed it.

A similar situation arose with respect to the technology that was being incorporated into our projects. The need to have immediate and constant feedback for our planning questions led to the formation of a sister company for technical systems integration – TEC:ton engineering. Besides a tighter integration process, and instant technical support, the close collaboration has had other benefits. A shorter path of communication and established ways to collaborate have increased the awareness of the different disciplines and made the integration of equipment and wiring easier over time. The ability to provide expanded services has sometimes helped us find the resources to refine and polish plans beyond what would otherwise have been possible.

The next step in the process of complete integration was the addition of a partnership with the construction company of a pre-eminent studio builder, Frank Latouf. Giving us the potential to provide design-build services, this association complements the roster of required services for the completion of any media production project.

Besides these ventures, which are all based on our direct involvement, looser associations with talented individuals and groups have been of great benefit to us. Ranging from manufacturing to publishing and even microchip design, the most important affiliations are described in more detail later on. And finally, to further expand what we see as an ongoing process of cross-disciplinary integration, we have begun setting up a structure that lets each of us focus on a particular area of expertise or preference, while fostering close collaboration.

To conclude, this book is not meant to be a textbook, or to present solutions and recipes for the design and engineering of these projects. It is not intended simply to answer questions posed by current technology or acoustical engineering. Nor is it overly concerned with the more elusive aspects of theory and philosophy. All the same, we hope it gives an overview of an area in contemporary building that has not yet been widely documented.

04

01

Most of all, we hope it demonstrates that what the scientist and thinker Edward O. Wilson calls "consilience," or the unity of knowledge, can be applied to practical uses in the fields in which we work. We would like to propose a holistic and comprehensive approach to design and engineering, where each discipline benefits from knowing something about the others. As different as many of the perspectives evoked here may be, there is ample room for the sharing of insights, and indeed inspiration, among them. While we enjoy the indisputable benefits of specialization, we must look for ways to counteract the accompanying fragmentation of knowledge by trying to understand more about other things.

And maybe architecture is frozen music after all.

Peter Grueneisen, Los Angeles 2003

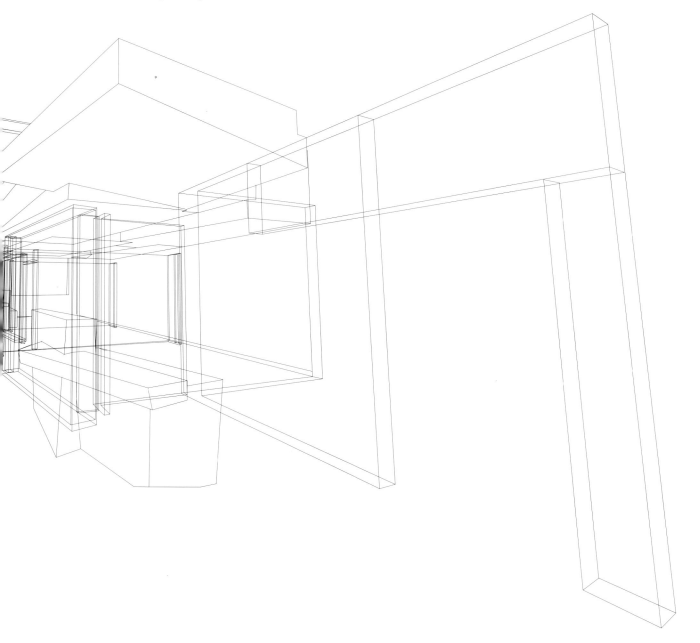

01 Antara Cold Storage Facility, Vietnam
02–03 Addition to R. Neutra's Freedman House, Pacific Palisades
04 Rockland Studios, Chicago

Neither science nor the arts can be complete without combining their separate strengths. Science needs the intuition and metaphorical power of the arts, and the arts need the fresh blood of science.

EDWARD O. WILSON

ARCHITECTURE / ART / TECHNOLOGY

SOUNDSPACE ARCHITECTURE FOR SOUND AND VISION

02.019

01

PROTRUDE, FLOW
Sachiko Kodama and Minako Takeno

Sachiko Kodama (*1970, Shizuoka Prefecture, Japan), graduated from Hokkaido University, 1995 M.A. University of Tsukuba – Art and Design, 2000 completed doctoral program University of Tsukuba – Art and Design, Minako Takeno (*1969, Tokyo, Japan), graduated from Tama Art University, 1995 M.A. University of Tsukuba Art and Design

CONCEPT

We are pursuing the creation of interactive installations to move our primitive feelings. Dynamic, organic shapes and the movement of the black, lustrous magnetic fluid express a passion for life. The phenomenon of the fluid rising against gravity reminds us of something living. The fluid moves according to the synchronous sound. These installations are not like machines, but remind us of the energy of pulsating liquid in the body of life.

PROTRUDE, FLOW

Modeling physical material more freely and making it move more flexibly is a dream long sought after by human beings, and many artists have created surreal illusions in pictures or moving images. But those were imaginary.

Can we obtain a real object that transforms itself as we have designed it? *Protrude, flow* is an interactive installation, which expresses the dynamics of fluid motion of physical material, the dynamics of organic, wild shapes and movements of liquid by means of digital computer control.

Protrude, flow uses magnetic fluid, sound, and moving images. Affected by the sounds in the exhibition space, the three-dimensional patterns of the black fluid transform in various ways, and its flowing movement and dynamic transformations are simultaneously projected on the wide screen.

The fluid appears occasionally as pointed mountains or pliable organic shapes, sometimes as flowing particle streams.

UNSTABLE VOLUMES

Brandon LaBelle

Brandon LaBelle is an artist and writer. He is the co-editor of *Writing Aloud: The Sonics of Language* and *Site of Sound: Of Architecture and The Ear*, published by Errant Bodies Press. He is currently a PhD candidate at the London Consortium researching the developments of sound art.

01

MEASURING THE ACOUSTICS BETWEEN MUSIC AND ARCHITECTURE

We think of buildings as generally keeping noise out, mini-mizing the amount of external stimuli that can get inside and cause disruption. The interior is protected as a sanctuary where one can feel at ease, away from the violent stirrings of the outside world, where quiet is a sought-after state, an envelope for the ear. This decibel war between interior and exterior finds its most extreme expression in military uses of high volume to torture an enemy psychologically. During the United States invasion of Panama the sound of Jimi Hendrix was used to drive Noriega out of hiding – to draw him into the open, and into custody. Thus, the United States interven-tion breached not only Panama's sovereign border but also the molecular stability of its air.

Yet listening can also save us from an outside, from an exter-nal force threatening the privacy of an interior state. The Hythe Sound Mirrors, architectural relics of the 20s and 30s along the southeast coast of England, were constructed as listening devices to help in the early detection of German bombers. The Mirrors were in effect an early form of radar, and a stage in the technological arms race. (Electronic radar would later be developed during the Second World War.) Large concrete walls and discs projecting out toward the sea, the Mirrors were used to collect the sound of bombers off the coast and relay them to a listener who sat below in a con-crete room with a pair of headphones, tuning in to the mys-terious murmurs of a sonic environment. Here, the state

border functions as a zone of audible terror, while the sensitive quiverings of the ear canal signal the difference between possible defense and mass destruction. The sensitivities of the ear canal are also at the core of a multitude of musical compositions, installations, projects and theories. The psycho-acoustic dimension in leading to a depth of experience, from the terrifying to the sublime, the soldier in the bunker to the listener on the brink of sleep, hovers as a sonic phenomenon that informs the historical lineages of the intersections of sound and architecture. For these intersections are based on the supposition that acoustic phenomena and spatiality are partially conceived and understood through the ability to perceive such phenomena, by stretching the ear beyond reason.

PRE-VIRTUAL VIRTUALITY

The perceiving of acoustic sounds at such a long distance requires a leap of imagination – in the telephonic relay the message of sound signifies according to a virtuality of meaning: one hears a sound (the German bomber, a police siren, etc.) and understands its information (air raid, public warning) without necessarily seeing the original source. In his ongoing study of the physical and psychological consequences of vehicular motion (speed), Paul Virilio describes this virtuality of "projection": "The speed of the new optoelectronic and electroacoustic milieu becomes the final void (the void of the quick), a vacuum that no longer depends on the interval between places or things and so on the world's very extension, but on the interface of an instantaneous transmission of remote appearances, on a geographic and geometric retention in which all volume, all relief vanish."[1] The Mirrors as early radar anticipate "the void of the quick" – the collapse of relief as the sounds of bombers at a distance are suddenly made apprehensible, within the fractional space of the listener's ear canal, in an instantaneous bolt of perception.

In tracing the line between architecture and music one butts up against obstacles – the very surfaces of buildings stand in the way, deflecting the sound wave; yet there are openings as well: acoustical reverberations find their way past the wall, seeping into the structure itself, and leading out, across open space.

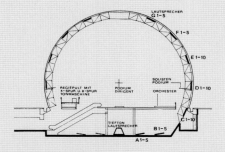

When describing the process behind *I Am Sitting in a Room* (1969) in an interview with Douglas Simon, the composer Alvin Lucier articulates a shift in his own sonic perception: "Thinking of sounds as measurable wavelengths, instead of as high or low musical notes, has changed my whole idea of music from a metaphor to a fact and, in a real way, has connected me to architecture."[2] For Lucier this "factual" presence of music as a measurable reality comes into being through an understanding of the interplay between sound and space. The work *I Am Sitting in a Room* consists of recording a speaking subject (Lucier) reading the score, which is itself a description of the actual process the work undertakes. Replaying this initial recording-speaking back into the space and re-recording it again and again, the initial recording is reduced to its tonal properties. In this way the acoustical properties of the room affect the recording (and voice) and demonstrate how one's location is always influencing what one hears. *I Am Sitting in a Room* pits the vocalizing subject and the idiosyncrasies of language as speech pattern (a unique sound source) against the acoustical characteristics of space – in this case, a room. What results is a recorded mutation through which the voice is deflected against space, transformed in an electromagnetic replay that melds the body of the subject with the body of architecture.

This dichotomy of sound and space, music and architecture, has a third point of concern. The ear acts as the final note in a triangular relation – not an apex but a perceptual link. In tracing this phenomenon one runs up against architecture AND music, buildings AND composition, engineering AND performance, and an overarching lineage of attempts to mingle the two: sound-sculpture, concert hall design, site-specific installation, urban design, art projects, happenings etc. Artists, architects, engineers, designers and composers have all traced this line themselves, initiating conversations between sound and space as a way of drawing attention to the interdependency of this relationship and the discrepancies that rupture their harmonious comingling. For what this work teaches us is that culture is always brimming with unexpected conversations which tease out the tensions between the imaginary and the experiential.

01–02 Sound Mirrors, Hythe, 1930
03–04 German Pavilion by Fritz Bornemann, Expo 1970, Osaka

For the 1970 World Expo in Osaka, Japan, the composer
Karlheinz Stockhausen had a concert hall built to specifications that would embrace the sonic character of his electronic compositions. (The sound system was designed by
David Tudor and Gordon Mumma.) Like the cathedrals of
medieval Europe whose Gothic verticality lifts Gregorian
chants up to God through extended reverberation, or the
low-level temples of Japan whose horizontality spreads out
across the horizon, filtering the Buddhist chant into the
landscape along with plumes of incense, Stockhausen's
architectural requirements strive to magnify sound and
carry it onto a cosmic plane (as do various moments of electronic music from Varèse to Theremin to Terry Riley). More
importantly, they reveal a sensitivity toward the concert
hall as a determining space for musical experience: how
sounds are performed and heard within space. In view of
the specific attributes of electronic music, Stockhausen felt
a new concert hall needed to be built, one which would be
conducive to this music's new "proportions."

Recent concert hall designs in Tokyo have garnered acclaim
from musicians and architects alike. Unprecedented for its
attempt to work scientifically in creating a perfectly acoustical concert hall, the Tokyo Opera City concert hall was designed with the help of computer-generated renderings of
space based upon acoustical measurements, such as reverberation time, bass ratio, acoustical texture and clarity. Com-
menting on the designs, the architect Takahiko Yanagisawa
espoused a science-driven architecture, claiming that in attempts to "assimilate nuances beyond description,"[3] such
as those of sounds in space, architecture depends upon scientific data and conclusions.

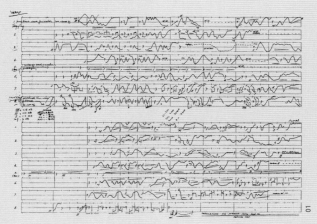

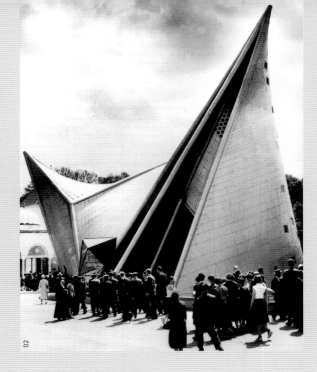

This constitutes a bio-genetic approach toward mapping
the molecular struggle between music and its performance,
deciphering the genome of Acoustics for the creation of the
Brave New Concert Hall. In the concert hall there are two
performances occurring: the playing of notes (presentation
of music) and the penetration of these notes into the ear
as defined by architectural space. To achieve fidelity we
must tweak space, for the ear is not necessarily a rational
organ, but is susceptible to its own "mood" swings, to internal agitations and slippages that frustrate and distort the
synaptic relay. In the psychology of acoustics the ear can
only be "imagined" as a stable referent, an absolute minus
the physical body. This necessitates an objectification of the
organ which, though it broadly succeeds in embodying its
own truth, nonetheless omits and blocks out hallucination,
feverish phantasy, mental disorders, and so on. In other
words, like all psychologies, acoustics is susceptible to the
unexplainable because it probes a depth that is always
slightly out of bounds.

Another highly original architecture-sound construction was
the Philips Pavilion (1958), built for the World's Fair in Brussels. The Philips Corporation commissioned the Swiss architect Le Corbusier to help highlight their latest technological
feats in audio equipment and image projection.[4] A kind of
early IMAX theater, the Philips Pavilion was a unique collaboration, bringing together Le Corbusier and Iannis Xenakis,
who worked in Le Corbusier's studio as a draughtsman and
engineer; also working on the Pavilion were the filmmaker
Philippe Agostini and the composer Edgard Varèse, whose
abiding interest in electronics found its ultimate fulfillment
in his composition *Poème Electronique* (amplified by the Pavilion's unprecedented use of modern speaker technology).
Much in the project is attributable to the engineering bril-
liance of Xenakis, who left the studio feeling abused by Le
Corbusier's unwillingness to give him due credit. For instance, some four hundred speakers were mounted into the
hyperbolic paraboloid structure (as devised by Xenakis with
reference to a *glissando*). With hidden film projectors shooting out multiple images across the curved walls, audiences
who attended the Pavilion were subjected to a 480-second
phantasmagoric narrative of sound and image celebrating the
technological future (or at least the Philips version of it).
Essentially, the Pavilion was supposed to be an architectural
and musical articulation of this future – a literal embodiment
of this new spatial experience of "virtuality."

THE BODY IN SPACE

In contrast to the Philips Pavilion and other early architectural projects of late Modernism that sought to bridge the gap between mass production and new media technologies (electronic virtuality), some contemporary artists have engaged with sound and space from a more personal perspective on the physical experience of everyday life. One such artist, Bernhard Leitner from Vienna, has been investigating architectural form since the late 1960s with the desire to create variations of auditory experience. His public sculptural projects of the last twenty years, which he more appropriately refers to as "sound-spaces," involve the building of structures that support psycho-acoustic experience in terms of acoustics while providing public, inhabitable space for such experience. Metal towers in rows or circles, rooms with hidden speakers in the walls that emit amplified audio recordings – dense drones that ricochet and deflect across space. For example, *Sound-Space* (1984), installed at the Technical University in Berlin, consisted of a square room whose walls were covered in acoustically absorbent metal material (a kind of membrane that holds sound rather than deflecting it), making environmental sounds somehow less imposing, hushed. Like Leitner's work in general, *Sound-Space* confronts a viewer-listener with its physical alterations of space – we recognize the shift in space through a psycho-acoustic disturbance. In this particular work, this shift is the absorption of sound – the room as a stifled space. Inside the walls forty-eight loudspeakers are mounted, amplifying given frequencies. The frequencies seep into the quiet space and at the same time are absorbed back into the walls, creating a highly active and self-reflective (even self-consuming) public space.

Public space is likewise of real importance to the artist Achim Wollscheid, whose art and music works since the early 1980s have investigated the dynamic of public space through musical concepts. In essence, music and architecture converse in Wollscheid's work, opening up the often hidden space where the two meet. His recent project for a specially constructed home in Gelnhausen by the architects Gabi Seifert and Götz Stöckmann exemplifies his ability to transform "sound-space" into forms that make architecture and music into the poles of a complex relationship.

Wollscheid's work is installed along the front wall and two sides of the house and consists of speakers and microphones mounted at the same points, with one inside and the other outside. Connecting the exterior microphone to the interior speaker, and the interior microphone to the exterior speaker, the work essentially amplifies outside sounds inside, and inside sounds outside. At the same time, however, a computer program transforms the sounds as information into tones. This phenomenal feed into an electronic equivalent – a relay between "street" and "living room" – frustrates the architectural imperative of an exterior-interior divide, insisting instead on a more "permeable" structure with a sonic view onto the unexpected. For here even the subtle intermingling of nature and architecture that someone like Wright pursued in his "organic architecture" (as perfectly exemplified by "Fallingwater" in Pennsylvania, where the presence of a waterfall is incorporated into the interior of the house) is disrupted. In contrast to the sought-after harmony of phenomenal occurrence (nature) and a cultural work (architecture/music), Wollscheid's project is an invitation to "noise," to potential disruption and play – here; the walls of a housewelcome the interference of an outside, while the private interior is amplified outwards to an unexpected public.

03-04

01 Edgard Varèse, *Poème Electronique*, 1957
02 Philips Pavilion, Expo 1958, Brussels
03–04 Achim Wollscheid, Project for House in Gelnhausen, Germany, designed by Gabi Seifert and Götz Stöckmann, 2003

01–02

HOME IS WHERE THE HEART IS

The house as a form occupies a deep place within the imagination. Freud's theory of the uncanny (*Unheimlich*) relates this feeling to the home: the literal meaning of *Unheimlich* is "unhomely," and Freud describes the uncanny as an experience in which the ordinary becomes haunted, is made strange by a set of special circumstances, a convergence of memory and imagination that draws hidden trauma out into the material space of the home. Inside, things suddenly don't feel right: the home is occupied by a foreign presence, pregnant with suspect murmurs. This psychological unease disrupts the private organization of the home.

Klaus Schuwerk and Francisco Lopez's *Tonhaus* is a house of listening, a place where resonance invades space through an elaborate architectural structure that opens itself up to the pervasion (and perversion) of sound (and the murmurs of the imagination). *Tonhaus*, a collaboration between architect and composer, is a design for a specially constructed concrete building equipped with a system of metal tubes that act as transmitters or conveyers of sound. Prepared recordings are channeled through the tubing system from a "control room" and spill out of perforations throughout the building. Designed to be located outside Madrid, *Tonhaus* extends the architecture of the ear out into the world, as an inhabitable space, making "sound part of the building, and the building part of the sound" (according to the liner notes from the CD release documenting the proposal). Listening is thus the focal point by which architecture is determined, and the subtle vibrations of resonance are a physical presence that undermines the interior-exterior split. Yet this concert hall is one whose structure itself is the instrument, vibrating from within through its own internal amplification system, rather than from airwaves hitting its surface.

The dimensions of the ear are also reflected in the work of Michael Brewster. Working in Los Angeles since the late 60s, Brewster has spent his time exploring sound as sculpture. The acoustic interplay of sound and space results in the static appearance of a sound whose volume is not perceptible solely by virtue of its audibility, but also as presence, weight, and mass.

Working with sine waves, Brewster has constructed a studio unlike any other: an empty, enclosed white room whose dimensions are designed to accentuate sound waves and, in essence, to bring its features into relief as sculptural form – as a weight bearing down on the body. Unlike La Monte Young's *Dream House*, where the space between ear and sound creates music with the turning of the head, Brewster is more interested in mapping the architecture of this space, the physicality in play between the ear-body and the sound-body: "Hearing is well suited to the tasks of sculpture. It occurs in the round, sensing all directions and dimensions simultaneously, unlike seeing which is frontal and singular in its attention. It is difficult to see a sculpture fully, it's always a bunch of sequenced frontalizations. If sculpture is to achieve its potential it ought to occur in the round, all around you, simultaneously."[5]

In mapping the space between the ear and architecture, the work of Max Neuhaus stands as a pivotal legacy, which continues to offer insight into the dynamics of sound and space as an extension of experimental music. After leaving behind his career as a percussionist in the mid-60s, Neuhaus began experimenting with different methods of overcoming the divides of the music world's conventional wisdom: audience vs. performer, instrument vs. amplification, score vs. interpretation, music vs. auditorium, etc. Neuhaus's artistic work overrides these splits in favor of a more immediate, psycho-acoustic and communal experience, which is only present as a site-specific occurrence. His early work, during the late 60s and early 70s, included radio broadcasts created by listeners calling in and triggering sounds, or the broadcasting of sounds recorded as one proceeds along a stretch of road – tuning into the radiophonic progression. Such experiments led Neuhaus into obscure terrain.

Probably one of the first artists to refer to his work as "sound installation," Neuhaus built on the relationship between sound and space, public/private, expansive/intimate – an interaction whose outcome can be thought of as "shades" of color varying in relation to one's own position. His work for Documenta IX in 1993, *Three to One*, is a sound installation involving three floors of an empty building. The work exploits the interplay of the three floors as separate yet interrelated spaces, and one experiences it as "layers" of sound-color: moving up the stairs, one leaves behind the "cool blue" of a quiet drone and ascends into an open space of deeper contrasts – the subtlety of mixing environments awakening the aural in a synesthetic way. Thus the building itself becomes a humming, vibratory structure.

REDEFINING SPACE

This new potential for form, for experience, be it architectural or musical, everyday or out of the ordinary, is indicative of an interdisciplinary approach. In the mingling of disparate media one recognizes relationships and connections between music and architecture, performance and urban design, installation and public space. And further, crossing the lines of different practices leads out onto perceptual shifts – between ethics and social policy, experience and activism, private and public responsibility. The architect Bruce Goff recognized this during his early training, when he published various journals in the 1920s, and asserted that there were important things to be learned from ALL the arts. Reflecting a growing sentiment of the times, from Frank Lloyd Wright to Moholy-Nagy, Goff's architectural work often refers to his interest in music. Some of his own early musical compositions were produced by hand-cutting patterns in piano rolls for player-pianos, creating a kind of "visual-sonic poem." Here the patterns of holes can be viewed more readily in terms of architectural layout and blueprint (the formation of a conception of space) than in terms of musical composition.

Goff's continued interest in music led to correspondence with Partch and Varèse, who in the 1950s exchanged letters with Goff on the "spatialization of music" – something Goff readily accepted. Probably Goff's most direct and eloquent way of connecting music and architecture was through teaching. As a professor at the University of Oklahoma, Goff would often use musical references such as "counterpoint" and "repetition" to describe architectural principles, inculcating a deep appreciation for musical ideas in his students.

The work of Paul Panhuysen shows how a musical practice can shape urban design and throw very basic conventions into question. His more overtly architectural work from the early to mid-70s reflects an overall interest in working directly with the very ordinary situation of "street life" – i.e. the street as a potential living space. His proposal for Wilgenroosstraat, Eindhoven, Holland asked that the street on which he was then living be turned into part-pedestrian area and part-garden. With trees running down the middle of the street, and cars parked behind houses, the work proposes the street as a communal space. This proposal of Panhuysen's reconfigures our understanding of the neighborhood, of how houses are constructed around the presence of the automobile. His whimsy opens up our perception of space, demonstrating the way in which architecture and urban design are based on seemingly immutable conventions, and once we are given this alternative vision space suddenly becomes a highly malleable form. This sense of community characterizes Panhuysen's work in general, but especially his twenty years as manager of the Apollohuis in Eindhoven. The Apollohuis was a space for presenting experimental audio work, both as installation and as performance. Now closed due to lack of funding, it was an extremely important venue, and greatly supportive as an institution of artists from around the world in their investigations of the sonic peripheries. Another project, the Apollo House, addresses the architectural necessity of housing artistic practice in general. Metaphorically, the cultural work of experimental audio needs its own space; as in the case of any artistic undertaking, literature or music, film or dance, space provides a framework in which the work can be received, made part of larger conversations and communities, integrated into systems of cultural reference. Space accommodates the work, offering much needed support for its ongoing development – in this instance, as an architecture where the idiosyncrasies of experimentation can be amplified.

[1] Paul Virilio, *Open Sky*, tr. Julie Rose
New York and London: Verso, 1997
[2] Alvin Lucier and Douglas Simon, *Chambers*,
Middletown, CT: Wesleyan University Press, 1980
[3] James Glanz, *Art + Physics = Beautiful Music*,
New York Times, 18 April 2000
[4] For a detailed account of the Philips Pavilion,
see Marc Treib's *Space Calculated in Seconds*,
Princeton, NJ: Princeton University Press, 1996.
[5] Michael Brewster, *Where, There or Here?*
in *Site of Sound: Of Architecture and the Ear*,
ed. Brandon LaBelle and Steve Roden,
Los Angeles: Errant Bodies Press, 1999

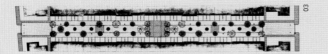

03

01 Michael Brewster, *An Exit to Sculpture*, Museum
of Contemporary Art, Los Angeles, 1985
02 Michael Brewster, *Concentrate – Break Up*, Tunnel to the beach
at the end of Taraval Street, San Francisco, 1977
03 Paul Panhuysen, Proposal for Wilgenroosstraat, Eindhoven, 1975

MAXIMUM DIRECTNESS

Wolf D. Prix / COOP HIMMELB(L)AU

Since 1993, Wolf D. Prix has been tenured Professor of Architectural Design; and since 1999 Dean of Architecture, Industrial Design, Product Design, Fashion and Stage Design at the Universität für Angewandte Kunst, Vienna. From 1984–2001 he taught at the Architectural Association in London; Harvard University in Cambridge; SCI-Arc and UCLA in Los Angeles. In 2001 Wolf D.Prix received a Doctor Honoris Causa de la Universidad de Palermo, Buenos Aires, Argentina.

01

Architecture and music have absolutely nothing to do with one another. COOP HIMMELB(L)AU and the Rolling Stones have absolutely nothing to do with one another. We are neither as famous nor as rich as the Rolling Stones, and unlike them we can't just do anything we want. What the Stones achieved with their music – playing against the trends, which they felt was important and right – meant a lot to us at the time we were forming our ideas about a new architecture.

COOP HIMMELB(L)AU was founded in 1968, at a time when not only architecture but everything was exploding. Art, science, technology, education, philosophy – and music. In May 1968, "All power to the imagination" was the message written on the walls of Paris. Connections – or networks, as we would say nowadays – were the key to expanding your vocabulary and your consciousness. We didn't take our model from the architecture of our forefathers, but from rock and pop culture. Fashion, the new philosophy, the dream of an anti-authoritarian society, and rock 'n' roll. Every week you'd hear a new group, and every day a new number. Cassius Clay/Muhammad Ali's boxing strategy served us as a model for urban planning. We weren't interested in what they'd built two hundred years ago, but in how an astronaut's helmet was made. The moon landing was almost an act of redemption, for it enabled us to see that the protective function of architecture was a thing of the past (looking back, I think we fatally overestimated the construction industry), and this insight opened the doors to architecture. At the time, our designs were not concerned with space, but with the experience of space. Media, light, smells, sounds, vivacity and rock 'n' roll. Action, shock, provocation, anything new, anything young.

The Stones were the forerunners of the new aesthetics: louder, more brutal, more shocking, more rebellious. *Beggars Banquet. Satisfaction.* And they were funny: "We don't wear ties, 'cos they dangle in our soup when we eat". This was a radical statement in 1964 – a desperate time. In rock 'n' roll, electric guitars and amplifiers allowed bands to express their feelings about life without mediation. A concept grips you the moment it is directly transported through the medium. For us, this meant that the livelier and more intense our building designs were, the livelier and more intense their impact was. We couldn't prove it, but we felt sure of it.

At the time, music – and with it all of architecture – was undergoing an incredible revolution. Everyone was influencing everyone else: the Stones, the Beatles, Cream, Dylan, Hendrix. Everything that was old was rejected and created anew. "Who wants yesterday's paper? Nobody in the world" – that was the motto. For us, too. Florian, himself a rock guitarist with Moon 44, pointed out possible parallels between the Stones and HIMMELB(L)AU when he saw our Falkestrasse project and spontaneously said: "That looks like Keith Richards' solo on *Gimme Shelter*." This doesn't mean that *Gimme Shelter* is constructed like a building or that we draw and build the way Richards plays the guitar. It's simply about the concept that comes across in both projects.

It is all too easy to forget that the Stones are an incredibly conceptual band, and that *Beggars Banquet* and *Exile on Main Street* are not only the names of architectural projects, but also albums with a concept structure. The way Keith Richards plays the rhythm guitar on *Under my Thumb* and *Sister Morphine* generates a tension comparable, metaphorically speaking, to the tension flow in our buildings. Basically, Keith's riffs are relatively simple variations on standard rock 'n' roll accompaniments. *Satisfaction* was nothing but a Chuck Berry riff with a slightly different rhythm.

The complex structures of our projects are devised in similar fashion. To make them calculable, they are deconstructed and reduced to their basic component parts, and they only reacquire their complexity once they are assembled. We were thus able to transfer Keith's style of playing metaphorically, but not literally, to our work.

And then there's his posture. You only have to see Keith Richards on stage to see how he almost deconstructs. The way he holds the guitar – hanging below his belt, like every good guitarist, because it feels better there – corresponds exactly to the flow of forces in our structures: an attempt to convert body language into architecture.

When the Rolling Stones' rhythm section gets going, you sometimes feel as if you're flying. Unfortunately, you can't create this feeling in architecture. What we can try to achieve in our architecture is greater directness, thus creating a similarity between our work and rock 'n' roll. The reduction and enrhythming of tension in music corresponds to the rhythm of tension in spatial sequences. We also felt a greater affinity to bands than to loners, because we were always asking ourselves: how do the Stones, the Beatles and Cream work? What are the necessary preconditions for teamwork? Dylan, a loner, was never an important point of reference for HIMMELB(L)AU.

We create our designs as a team, just as the Stones did with their track *Sympathy for the Devil* in the film *One Plus One*. The guitarist has a vague idea; it's far from taking shape. The singer says yes, well, okay – but why don't we add an A minor chord there? And then the drummer starts playing in the background, the bass joins in, and you have a new number. And we don't sit around all on our own either, committing solitary, brilliant ideas to paper.

In 1968–69, there was always music playing while we were drawing, and it was usually the Stones. *Gimme Shelter* was effectively the official HIMMELB(L)AU anthem. When Michael Pilz made the first TV film about us in 1970, the music was taken from *Gimme Shelter*. Later, we chose the number *Sympathy for the Devil* for our action with the *Flammenflügel (Burning Wing)*. Everyone asked us why we hadn't chosen the *Einstürzende Neubauten*. Our answer was, and still is, very simple: there is a concept behind the Stones' number, it is developed and fades out as a concept. The tracks by *Einstürzende Neubauten* are pure show.

In the mid-70s we lost sight of the Stones. Their old tracks were no longer so important to us during this period, when we had come to see our architecture as a counter-strategy to all the tarting-up and smoothing-over of actual content, to all the monstrous pleasantness then in vogue.

The Stones also became pleasant. In the early days they were still hard and rough, but then they adapted to the spirit of the times and became increasingly trivial, until they ended up merely putting on a show, just like, say, Pink Floyd with *The Wall*. That was when we lost interest. I still listen to the old Stones tracks from time to time. But I soon get bored – unless I listen to them analytically. How did they play that stuff in the old days? How come they had so much drive?

01 Keith Richards, Amsterdam, 1998
02 Falkestrasse, Vienna, Project 1984–89
03 UFA Cinema Center, Dresden, Project 1998
04 Klangturm, Expo 02 Biel, Project 2002
05 Mick Jagger and Keith Richards, Boston, 2002

:: ARCHITECTURE ART TECHNOLOGY / WOLF D. PRIX

SOUNDSPACE ARCHITECTURE FOR SOUND AND VISION

SOUND BOX SOUND

Daniel Ott with Roderick Hönig, Peter Niklas Wilson and Peter Zumthor

Daniel Ott (*1960, Grub/Appenzell) – composer, pianist – theater studies in Paris and London – study of composition in Essen and Freiburg – in 1990, founded the "contemporary music *rümlingen*" festival – since 1995, teaches experimental music at the University of the Arts in Berlin.

RODERICK HÖNIG
DANIEL OTT
PETER ZUMTHOR

CONCEPT

The Swiss Pavilion at Expo 2000 is first and foremost an experience for the senses. Architecture, Lightscripts, Music, Drinking, Eating, and Sound Box Clothing combine to form a *Gesamtkunstwerk* organized and sustained by the tension of an invisible mise-en-scène. Throughout Expo 2000, this performance will undergo continual change and renewal and will also adjust to visitor numbers, the season, and weather conditions. The architectural and musical compositions, literary texts, musicians and hosts, gastronomy and apparel, all are Swiss or are relevant to Switzerland. Visitors to the Sound Box will be able to recognize the references being made, enter into conversations to find out more about them, and if necessary find out even more. But not just this, and not predominantly this either: foremost is Switzerland as a cultured hostess. Switzerland's appearance is not didactic: there are no advertising messages, no self-criticism, no self-appraisal and no gratuitous self-indulgence. The Swiss Pavilion offers visitors suffering from media overload and exhibition fatigue a place to rest for a moment. It is a place of relaxation; a place that invites visitors to stroll about, to let go, to enjoy and discover.

BASIC STRUCTURE
The pavilion is based on four sets of parallel-stacked walls grouped around an open square in a pin-wheel-like formation. By extending this basic arrangement into a regular fabric-like pattern, an ordering concept is obtained which is used to generate the floor plan of the Sound Box. The visitor experiences the Sound Box in spatial terms like a labyrinth, a series of walls running parallel and perpendicular to one another containing small internal voids (cross courts and flanked courts). The intertwining stacked walls are reminiscent of the weave and warp of textiles: all the stacked walls running north-south are made from larch, all those running east-west from Douglas fir.

RESONANCE CHAMBER
The spatial and structural engineering is designed to amplify and direct the tone and timbre of the commissioned musical compositions. The image of a large sound-box was used as a basis for the design. The acoustic properties of the structure could not be calculated in advance but had to be intuitively felt. The interplay between architectural construction, acoustic space and various musical sounds was tested in Chur using sound trials on a full-scale sample stack. During the tests it was discovered that the dulcimer (second only to the accordion in the production of the basic sound), has a structure markedly similar to that of the Sound Box.

MUSIC
Music is a non-stop feature of the Sound Box, involving some three hundred fifty musicians from all around the world. All cultural regions of Switzerland are represented. Twelve musicians work in three-hour shifts from 9:30 am to 9:30 pm.

The musical concept devised by Daniel Ott comprises the basic sound, improvised passages and the so-called music windows c|–. The basic sound is played by three accordionists and three dulcimer players. Through the use of infinitely variable elements, the basic sound responds to the principle of variation that underlies the architecture of the Sound Box.

BASIC SOUND
This is composed of 153 sounds (A, B 1–3, G 1–17, etc.) and 23 eruptions (16/9, 22/3, etc.). The sounds tend to spread out in space – a timbre that meanders through the room. The eruptions are loud, shrill, rhythmic, non-linear and aperiodic. Basic sounds and eruptions appear alternately in a shifting pattern, based on a different schedule every day. During rehearsals in the spring of 2000, the existing or pre-composed sounds were customized for the Sound Box, a process in which almost all of the musicians took part. During these rehearsals in Hanover, the staging and musical vocabulary of the Sound Box was enhanced by the ideas of the participating musicians. The musicians might therefore be called joint composers.

IMPROVISED PASSAGES
In addition to the six basic sound musicians, three improvising musicians perform on a daily basis. They react with a variety of instruments to the basic sound: they improvise, engage with it, disrupt or denounce it, comment on it, complement and question it – all in an attempt to broaden the musical horizon.

MUSIC WINDOWS
Along with the basic sound and the improvised passages, this is the third element of the musical concept. The musicians performing in the music windows play "as they would at home" for short periods of between thirty seconds and two minutes. Depending on the musicians' musical background, their association with a particular music scene and their native folk music, the windows may produce sounds that are jazzy, noisy, folksy, original, eccentric, etc.

COMPOSITION METHOD
For the music in the Swiss Sound Box, Daniel Ott wanted to find a method that would allow him to prolong the actual composing of the music over a long period of time – permitting frequent interruptions in order to manage the sounds and contact musicians to discuss this amazing project. Together they researched various sounds and conducted sound rehearsals in the sample stack and in the Sound Box during its shell stage. The resulting Sound Box music consists of heterogeneous building blocks that can be reconfigured daily during the 153-day performance. Ott began to compose individual parts, so-called Day Projects, within one day: 22/3, 16/9, 19/12, 29/1, 26/5.

NUMBERS IN MUSIC
The same numbers were used for the Sound Box Music and again for the timing of interval structures. The time structure, based on seconds, timing or tone chains and pauses, produces rows of numbers/proportions; just like counting half-tone intervals. Here, the composer has attempted to convert the numbers that he gathered from the Sound Box enterprise into a composition and then convert the rows of numbers and proportions produced by the composition into sounds and time-based structures. For example, the time-based dimension (153 exhibition days: 153 sounds; 23 exhibition weeks: 23 eruptions); or architectural numbers: twelve stacks, three courts, the number of beam layers within a stack (4, 5, 6, 8, 10 or 11), proportions of the floor plan, etc.

:: ARCHITECTURE ART TECHNOLOGY / DANIEL OTT WITH RODERICK HÖNICK, PETER NIKLAS WILSON, PETER ZUMTHOR

SOUNDSPACE ARCHITECTURE FOR SOUND AND VISION

01–03 Swiss Pavilion, Expo 2000, Hanover

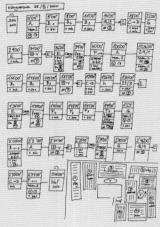

PETER NIKLAS WILSON
SPECULATION AND SPONTANEITY

Sounds created especially for space; known as Bodies of Sound. The typical Body of Sound has a long history in European music. One only has to think of Guillaume Dufay's motet *Nuper rosarum flores*, in which the essential proportions of the Cathedral of Florence were enciphered, this being played at the inauguration of the building itself. Returning to the near present, World Fairs have continually delivered probative occasions for special and spectacular combinations of sound and space. Anno Domini 1958 proved to be just such an occasion: 425 loudspeakers were set up in the Philips Pavilion at the World's Fair in Brussels out of which Edgard Varèse's four-channel *musique concrète opus, Poème électronique* sounded. In strict terms, however, a completely different kind of music would have been more obvious. That is, if Iannis Xenakis, at the time assistant to the nominal pavilion architect Le Corbusier, has chosen to base the bold lines of the building's architecture alone on the glissando scales of *Metastasis*, his scandalous Donaueschingen piece of 1955. It was in his *Polytope* project that Xenakis first managed to elevate space and sound concepts to the point where they formed a personal union.

A World Fair formed the background for Karlheinz Stockhausen to do the same once again in 1970, in Osaka, Japan. His works were played over 183 days, for five and a half hours each day, by a company of twenty musicians in a circular auditorium designed by Stockhausen himself. Nevertheless, the relationship between space and music

01, 06–07 Swiss Pavilion, Expo 2000, Hanover
02–05 Daniel Ott, Composition 22/3, Sample Composition Basic Sound, Composition 16/9, Procedural Sketch Sound Test, 1999–2000

remained rigid for Xenakis and Stockhausen alike: either a piece of music composed for space, or space created for a particular piece of music. Dynamic interaction was not seen to occur. Alvin Lucier delivers impressive models of the nature of this and how sound and Body of Sound can be made to merge into continually regenerating interrelationships. One instance of this is his *I Am Sitting In A Room* (1970), which takes the form of gradual metamorphosis from language to pure sound under the premise of each respective spatial resonance; another is *Vespers* (1968), an acoustic penetration of space using portable fathometers.

Completely different, yet equally plausible, concepts for dissolving rigid space-sound relationships originate from the free improvisation of music that developed out of the formal process of erosion of free jazz at exactly this time. It is not true that the least strength of authentic improvised music lies in its not existing in space as a finished product (or at best gradually adapting itself to space), but that it is formed out of the juxtaposition of silence, initially growing within space and then conforming to the character of space itself. Hardly any form of strange architectonic construction still exists that has not been acoustically reconnoitred by musical improvisers, be it a cathedral, an underground car park, a water tank, the interior of a dam – or even the Pyramids.

Daniel Ott's Body of Sound takes up aspects of all these diverse space-sound traditions and transcends them. The speculative-mathematical moment of joint sound-space proportions is doubtless present – and yet, at the same time, Ott's concept is open to the moment, open to the individuality of the musicians, and open to the idiom that resonates through them.

The more recognizable the contours and textures of the sound-architecture, the more room for maneuver they offer the guest musicians. It will never be hard to recognize who the conceptualist is behind this manifold event, yet this sound-construction has a sufficient number of doors to welcome and accommodate everything from free jazz to folk music, from a wide variety of origins. In relation to all of this, Daniel Ott's music is just as stringent, just as inviting, just as consistent, just as flexible, just as refined and just as unpretentious as Peter Zumthor's wooden construction.

The pavilion and the universe of sound that it produces now belong to the past. However, Ott's modular system of static regions of sound, motoric interspersions, and interpolated (in the form of an additional layer of sound) additive improvisations prove to be quick and morphic beyond the larch and pine beams of the Hanover pavilion.

02

SILOPHONE

[The User] – Thomas McIntosh and Emmanuel Madan

Silophone was created by [The User] and presented by Quartier Ephémère, the Société des arts technologiques, the Chaîne culturelle Radio-Canada with the technical collaboration of Bell and the support of the Canada Council for the Arts, the Daniel Langlois Foundation for Art, Science and Technology, the Port of Montreal and Mackie Designs.

Silophone is the sonic inhabitation of Silo #5, a massive abandoned grain elevator in the Port of Montreal. Silophone is a hybrid between virtual network and physical object. It uses various telecommunications technologies to introduce sounds collected from around the world into the stunning sonic space inside Silo #5 and to reflect the resulting echoes back to their senders.

The Silo itself is a vast complex composed of 115 vertical storage chambers, each 30 meters tall and up to 8 meters in diameter. The structure constitutes a sonic environment with extraordinary acoustic properties, most notably a reverberation time of over 20 seconds. Sounds occurring inside the building are dramatically transformed by these unusual acoustics.

[The User] has made the acoustic space of the Silo accessible to the outside world in four different ways:

The Sonic Observatory is a public sound installation located directly in front of Silo #5. It is constructed of reinforced concrete and equipped with a microphone and two speakers, inviting passersby to speak or sing into the Silo and simultaneously hear the results.

01–04 Silo #5, Exterior, Interior and Section, Montreal

A telephone exchange developed in collaboration with Bell Labs was designed to provide access to the Silophone via telephone. Callers are connected to a conference call, literally inside one of the giant storage bins in the Silo. They can use the telephone to send and receive sounds in real time. Two callers can speak and listen at once and up to thirty others can listen.

The Silophone website – www.silophone.net – allows users both to listen to the sonic activity inside Silo #5 and to contribute to it themselves. Visitors to the website select sound files from a database and broadcast them into the Silo. They may also add new sounds to the database, thus making them available for others to play. The resulting echo is sent back to them and to all other listeners through a Realaudio stream.

A series of works was commissioned from twenty-four local and international artists who were invited to play and to compose for the Silophone instrument. The compositions were presented during a series of concerts which took place directly in front of the building and at various locations in Montreal and in cities throughout the world, connected to the Silophone via network technology.

Given that the public cannot be admitted to Silo #5, first-hand experience of the building's acoustics is impossible. This implies that Silophone is a project about representation, relying exclusively on communications technologies to deliver mediated experiences to listeners and participants. Nevertheless, the project remains fundamentally rooted in an undeniably physical structure, namely, an enormous concrete grain elevator. Silophone's basis in both physical and virtual domains results in a hybrid space, which depends on both of its constituent elements for its existence. During the life of this project, sound artists and members of the public are invited to explore and help shape this realm.

The Silophone instrument is a collaborative work between [The User], who conceived and developed the three different access modes to the silo's interior, and the public, who employ these access modes. Public participation is central to our conception of the project: Silophone is entirely dependent upon that participation and cannot be considered complete without it. This principle of public access is a direct reaction to the lack of public urban policy that threatens the building.

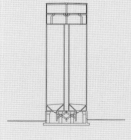

03

The sonic environment of Silophone functions on a temporal scale completely different from conventional "music," evolving over months and years rather than minutes or hours. We have referred to it as a year-long composition (indeed, it has now surpassed that duration). Additionally, rather than being the product of a single compositional intention, thousands of composers and performers have a hand in its making. As Silophone is continuously active, none of these composers or performers is involved for the entire lifespan of the piece; most contribute sonic material only once, while others may drop in regularly over a longer period of time. Similarly, no single listener has heard or will ever hear the entire composition.

This decentralized form of composition or sound-making results from the emphasis on active participation described above, as distinct from passive reception. Instead of presenting an audio recording or video document about Silo #5 to an audience as a finished work, we chose to disrupt the conventional boundaries between creator and audience. Consequently, our contribution to Silophone has not been the content but the container: it was central to the concept that the development of content should remain outside our control, so as to see what social, sonic, or musical phenomena might spontaneously occur. By deliberately setting up a public sonic space almost entirely devoid of rules and restrictions, we consciously ran many risks: uninteresting content, cacophony, or indeed simply silence. As it happens, silence did not often occur: close to 10 000 sound files have been deposited in Silophone's web archive, and the sonic observatory has channeled hundreds of thousands of vocal and other performances into the Silo. The most gratifying results of the Silophone experiment have been the hints of music that have begun to appear amid the noise.

The evolution of North America's economy from industrial to post-industrial has caused a dramatic shift in our society's perception of its industrial installations. The presence of heavy, production-based industry in the city center, which dates back to the continent's industrial heyday and culminated in the 1950s and 1960s, is perceived today as an outmoded and undesirable urban model.

:: ARCHITECTURE ART TECHNOLOGY / THOMAS McINTOSH AND EMMANUEL MADAN

The rise of the information-based economy in North America has been accompanied by a gradual exodus of the production-based industrial infrastructure to other continents, largely Asia and South America. What industry remains in the big cities of the North American continent has been largely relocated from the city center to the periphery. The port facilities of our major cities are particularly affected by this shift in perception to the point where, to many, the words "port" and "harbourfront" have become synonymous with leisure and tourism as opposed to industrial activity. Urban grain elevators are uniquely situated on a "fault line" between a resource-oriented industrial past and a present associated with the culture of leisure. Since the 1980s, Montreal's surviving grain elevators have been the uneasy neighbors of government-led initiatives emphasizing the new industries of leisure and tourism. Often these elevators are deemed too anachronistic for transformation and are simply destroyed. This redevelopment, along with similar revitalizing strategies in other North American cities such as Toronto, Vancouver and New York, shares a basic indifference to the very specific nature and history of the buildings upon which they impose a completely foreign program in a relatively short period of time.

The results of this kind of urban renewal can be seen increasingly throughout the post-industrial world: inadvertent, incongruous, surreal juxtapositions place shiny temples to the new deities of consumerism and leisure alongside relics of heavy industry and the production age. It is within this bizarre aesthetic landscape and the context of uneasy coexistence that the Silophone project chooses to situate itself.

Without becoming a proponent of industrial heritage conservation for its own sake, Silophone makes a proposal which is sensitive to and dependent upon the site it occupies. The inhabitation of an abandoned structure with sound offers a metaphor for a different approach to the re-integration of buildings into the urban fabric. It proposes something new which neither ignores nor destroys, but appropriates and is defined by this relic of the industrial age. In contrast to the "mega-project" approach, characterized by the speedy application of a foreign program, Silophone lays the groundwork for a gradual transformation of the building, growing a program to suit the container.

SOUNDSPACE ARCHITECTURE FOR SOUND AND VISION

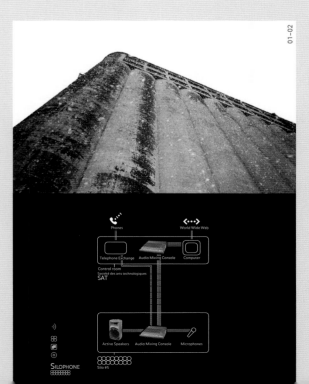

01–02

The Silophone website, www.silophone.net, was created with the technical and design expertise of Simon Piette and Étienne Désautels. Silophone's telephone interface, +1/514 844 5555, was developed in collaboration with Bell Canada's DATEC Emerging Technologies laboratories. [The User] also wishes to thank the many individuals who contributed to Silophone. Special thanks to Virginie Pringuet.

01, 04 Silo #5,
02 Technical Diagram, 2000
03 Silo #5, Closing Concert, June 2001

SOUNDSPACE ARCHITECTURE FOR SOUND AND VISION

04

01–02

ACOUSTICS IN CRITICAL LISTENING ROOMS

Bob Hodas

Bob Hodas travels the world helping studios normalize their rooms. His clients include Abbey Road Studios, Skywalker Ranch and studio bau:ton.

As an engineer and consultant, I have had the opportunity to work in a wide variety of control rooms around the world. In my experience, each one is unique. I would describe the concept of "tuning" a control room as the process one must follow in order to normalize the speakers for the space in which they are installed. By normalization, I mean creating a neutral acoustic signature, so that the finished music mix will translate properly when played on the wide variety of speaker systems in homes, cars, boom boxes etc. This is a three-part process involving speaker positioning, acoustic treatments, and if necessary equalization. The "audiophile" consumer may implement the same process to reproduce the music as heard by the producer and engineer.

SYMMETRY AND SPEAKER PLACEMENT
For Dustin Hoffman, in the movie *The Graduate*, the word of advice was "plastics." For studios the word is "symmetry." Not only should the room design itself be symmetrical, but the placement of the equipment or furniture is also critical in order to get the bass response correct for all speakers. Speakers must be placed symmetrically in a room or they will have different frequency responses. This means that music will sound different in the left and right speakers, the center image will be off-center, and the depth and soundstage will be collapsed and unbalanced. Proper phase alignment of the speaker components with respect to the listener is essential too for accurate music reproduction.

Most speakers are designed to have a linear frequency response in an anechoic environment. When a speaker is placed in a room with boundaries (walls), the bass response will start to change significantly. Bass response will build up even more when a speaker is placed against the wall (half-space loading) or in a corner (quarter-space loading). Why is this true? Below 200 Hz, speakers are fairly omni-directional. The sounds that bounce off the room boundaries mix in with the direct speaker signal. This delayed bounce will cause comb filtering. The time delay, and thus the frequency of interaction is dependent on the speakers' distance from the walls. If the left and right speakers are at different distances from the walls, the cancellations will occur at different frequencies. This is also true for first-order reflections above 400 Hz. Figures 03 and 04 demonstrate what happens to the bass when speakers are placed asymmetrically in a room.

03–04

ACOUSTIC TREATMENTS

When sound reflections from the ceiling, floor, and/or walls bounce back into the listener's position within about 19 milliseconds of the direct signal, the human brain cannot tell the difference between a direct and a reflected signal, and it all appears to come directly from the speaker. This causes phase problems, destructive comb filtering and thus cancellations in the frequency response. The result is imaging problems as well as frequency information loss. These undesirable boundary reflections can often be acoustically treated and minimized for the mid-to-high frequencies, but are more problematic on the low side. A well-designed room will use dimensions and wall angles that eliminate first-order reflections and minimize low-frequency mode build-up. Above 400 Hz, sound acts very much like light, so simple geometry (ray tracing) can be applied to identify the high-frequency reflections.

There are two choices for treating these reflections: absorption and diffusion. For the side walls and ceiling, absorption is recommended. An absorber removes the energy, but a diffusor spreads out the energy in space and time by generating many smaller reflections of lesser energy. For first-order reflections, an absorber demonstrates good coherence because the offending reflection has been removed. The diffusor's coherence reading is not good, because the reflection energy still reaches the mix position, creating a phase smear in the direct signal.

Absorption should be used sparingly, as it is easy to damp the high-end reverb time disproportionately. Just the areas that are problematic should be treated with a surgical attitude. There is nothing worse than the chesty sound of an over-absorbed room.

For the back wall, diffusion is preferred over absorption unless the back wall is closer than six feet to someone's head. Diffusion at the back opens up the sound of a small room, and the back-wall energy does not affect the coherence adversely.

Addressing low-frequency problems is a much more difficult issue. The use of broadband bass traps in the rear of the room has been popular and effective for many years. This is a good solution for stereo rooms since it can remove the back wall reflections that cause peaks and dips in the frequency response. With the development of 5.1 surround-sound monitoring, more precise traps must be used. The broadband traps are not effective since they remove too much bass from the rear speakers. Room designs are becoming more symmetrical front to back to accommodate the additional rear speakers, and treatments are following suit. Surgical use of membrane absorbers can deal with the offending frequencies; they also take up less space than the broadband approach.

EQUALIZATION

Equalizable room/speaker interaction is a minimum phase, second-order phenomenon exhibiting constant bandwidth and linear frequency spacing. Minimum phase frequency response anomalies occur when speakers are placed in proximity to boundaries such as walls and ceilings, or in soffits.

There is general agreement that an acoustic solution to a room problem is preferable to an EQ-only solution. However, if acoustic solutions are impractical or fail to cure a room's problems, then equalizers are called for. Ninety-five percent of the control rooms I have seen use equalizers for "tuning" the speakers in the room.

A parametric equalizer allows the user to dial in the exact center frequency and bandwidth curve necessary to address the problem. Figure 05 demonstrates the point. (Note that the green EQ curve is an inverse of the EQ being applied. This simply makes it easy to see how it fits into the room curve.) A parametric equalizer allows us to achieve a precision match to the room problem when teamed up with a high-resolution room analyzer.

Many audio professionals assume, not unreasonably, that the whole purpose of room tuning, whether acoustically or through EQ, is to make the room linear with respect to amplitude – i.e. "flat." Recording engineers do not in fact want a flat room. Experience shows that a flat room has no personality and is not fun to work in. Equally important, working in a flat room does not necessarily ensure a recording that sounds good in the outside world. While we want the system to be accurate, studio speakers typically have a "personality" that varies a bit from a linear response.

A gentle, linear roll-off starting in the upper mid-range has evolved into a working standard. High frequency loss due to tape aging, tape machine residual magnetization and high decibel listening levels for an extended time were the factors which led to this curve. Also, certain standards, such as the Dolby X-Curve, require an equalizer in order to compensate for the high-frequency loss due to movie screens and theater size.

As regards the low-frequency curve, most people prefer a slight bump in the bottom end. This gives the impression of a larger space, which is associated with a longer reverb time. Most concert halls exhibit this sort of low bump. Between the high/low personality filter, the best results throughout the midrange are achieved with a linear or flat tuning.

As speakers age, their resonant frequencies change and the room/speaker tuning will "drift" out. How long that takes depends on how often and how loud a system is driven. The use of equalizers allows us to maintain a standard of performance for the control room.

:: ARCHITECTURE ART TECHNOLOGY / BOB HODAS

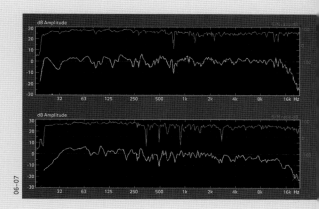

01–02 Test measurements of a room with good frequency response, compared to a room with very uneven sonic qualities
03–04 Left and right speaker asymmetrically placed in a room
05 Parametric EQ correction of low-end problem (inverse of EQ shown)
06–07 Room tuned flat (linear) versus room with sonic personality due to bass boost and slight roll-off of the higher frequencies

OUDE KERK

WORLD TRADE CENTER I

RESONANCE^3

Jeff Talman

Composer and sound installation artist Jeff Talman's investigations expose otherwise undetectable phenomena that inseparably connect sound and space.

By using recorded silence, he maps the inherent room tones of a space to then create site-specific compositions from the minute events captured. The specific reflexive qualities of these rooms, isolated from any external distractions, serve as the basis and the generator of a three-dimensional sonic architecture that captures their absolute spatial and acoustic essence. While the resulting sounds have been called "bewildering", "exquisitely muted" and "heavenly", the visual graphic output obtained through further processing, achieves a serene beauty on its own. Jeff Talman lives in New York and is represented by Bitforms.

01 Oude Kerk, Amsterdam 2002
02 World Trade Center I 2002
03 Resonance^3, Sound Installation at Bitforms Gallery, New York 2002

The centers of the walls, moreover, should be enriched by cornices of fine woodwork or white stucco, exactly halfway up. Without these cornices, the voices of those debating in the senate house, carried upward, cannot be understood by their listeners. But when the walls are encircled by cornices, the voice, as it rises from below, will be delayed before it carries upward on the air and dissipates; it will be intelligible to the ears. [...]

It is also important to note carefully that the site itself not deaden sound; it should be the type in which the voice may travel with the utmost clarity. This can be accomplished if a site is selected where resonances are not impeded. The voice is a flowing breath of air, and perceptible to the hearing by its touch. It moves by the endless formation of circles, just as endlessly expanding circles of waves are made in standing water if a stone is thrown into it. These travel outward from the center as far as they can, until some local constriction stands in the way, or some other obstacle that prevents the waves from completing their patterns. As soon as these obstacles interfere, the first waves bounce back and upset the patterns. In the same way the voice makes circular motions; however, on the surface of water the circles move horizontally, while the voice at once advances horizontally and mounts upward, step by step. For the voice, therefore, just as for the pattern of waves in water, so long as no obstacle interferes with the first wave, it will not upset the second wave or any of those that follow; all of them will reach the ears of the spectators without echoing, those in the lowermost seats as well as those in the highest. Therefore the architects of old, following in Nature's footsteps, perfected the stepped seating of theaters after their reaches into the rising of the voice. They asked how, using the canonical theory of mathematicians and the

BASIC ACOUSTICS

principles of music, any voice onstage might reach the ears of the spectators more clearly and sweetly. For just as musical instruments achieve the clarity of their sounds by means of bronze panels or horn sounding boxes added to the sound of the strings, so, too, the calculations for theaters were established by the ancients on harmonic principles to amplify the voice.

VITRUVIUS

HISTORY

SOUND AND ARCHITECTURE		
	PREHISTORIC TIMES	Sound in the natural field
Influenced by topography, vegetation		Temples, natural amphitheaters
	GREECE	Theaters, circuses Built-in resonant vessels
	ROME	
Gregorian Chant Plainchant	MIDDLE AGES	Gothic cathedrals Long reverberation times
	RENAISSANCE	Taj Mahal, Agra, India 1653 Reverberation time 28 seconds
Bach, Handel, Vivaldi, Corelli	1600 – 1750 BAROQUE	Small theaters, ballrooms, music rooms Shorter reverberation times
		Concert halls Opera houses Public venues
Haydn, Mozart, Beethoven	1750 – 1820 CLASSICAL	Grosser Musikvereinssaal Vienna 1870 Festspielhaus Bayreuth 1876 Concertgebouw Amsterdam 1888 Symphony Hall Boston 1900
Chopin, Liszt, Verdi, Puccini	1820 – 1900 ROMANTIC	Philharmonie Berlin (Hans Scharoun) 1963 Meyerson Symphony Hall Dallas (I.M. Pei) 1989
Stravinsky, Debussy, Varèse, Penderecki, Ligeti, Cage	20TH CENTURY	Concert Hall Lucerne (Jean Nouvel) 1999 Disney Concert Hall Los Angeles (Frank Gehry) 2003 [01]
Blues, Jazz, Rock 'n' Roll, Hip Hop Club Music World Music		Recording studios Very short reverberation times

[01]

ACOUSTIC SCIENCE		MEDIA TECHNOLOGY MILESTONES	
6th CENTURY BC		1806	Vibrations recorded on wax drum, no playback (Thomas Young)
Music and mathematics, vibrating strings (Pythagoras)		1857	Phonoautograph transcripts, no playback (Leon Scott de Martinville)
3rd CENTURY BC		1876	Invention of the telephone, microphone (Alexander Graham Bell)
Acoustic principles, sound propagation (Aristotle)		1877	Plans for a recording and playback machine, not built (Charles Cros)
1st CENTURY AD		1877	Paraffin paper phonograph (Thomas Edison)
De Architectura Libri Decem (Ten Books on Architecture) (Marcus Vitruvius Pollio)		1887	Wax cylinders (Thomas Edison)
		1888	Gramophone (Emile Berliner)
16th CENTURY		1894	Radio invented (Guglielmo Marconi)
Music for specific buildings (Adrian Willaert)		1897	Shellac records
		1902	Enrico Caruso's first recordings with acoustic recording horn, Victrola
17th CENTURY		1909	"Nutcracker", Tchaikovsky, first record album
Room acoustic principles (Athanasius Kircher)		1910	Patent for simultaneously reproducing movements and sound (Eugene A. Lauste)
Sound requires a medium (Robert Boyle)			
New Sciences (Galileo Galilei)		1912	Vacuum tube invented (Lee de Forest)
		1913	Kinetophone (Thomas Edison)
18th CENTURY		1916	Sound-on-film developed (Theodore Case)
Term "acoustics" introduced (Joseph Saveur)		1919	Theremin invented, first electronic instrument (Leon Theremin)
		1920	Commercial radio station (KDKA)
Speed of sound (Pierre Simon Laplace)	1816	1922	"The Audion" experimental animated sound-on-disc film (Western Electric)
Limits of hearing (Felix Savart)	1830		
Isoacoustic curve (John Scott Russell)	1839	1925	Electrical amplification (Bell Laboratories)
Precedence effect discovered (Joseph Henry)	1850	1926	"Don Juan" feature film premier (Vitaphone system)
Heinrich Hertz	1857	1927	Fully electronic television picture (Philo T. Farnsworth)
On the Sensations of Tones (Hermann Ludwig Ferdinand von Helmholtz)	1863	1928	"The Jazz Singer" full-length movie with synchronized sound (Warner Brothers)
The Theory of Sound (J.W. Strut – Lord Rayleigh)	1877	1929	33-1/3 rpm discs (RCA)
Fogg Museum Lecture Hall (Wallace Clement Sabine)	1895	1930	Bing Crosby's first solo record
Boston Symphony Hall (Wallace Clement Sabine)	1900	1931	EMI Studio at Abbey Road opens
Acoustics of Buildings (Floyd Watson)	1923	1932	"Poem of Fire" by Scriabin, first stereophonic recording (Leopold Stokowski)
Sound transmission loss calculations (Edgar Buckingham)	1925		
Anechoic chamber (Floyd Watson)	1927	1939	Magnetic tape invented
Sound level meter (Paul Sabine)	1930	1940	"Fantasia" animated movie, multi-channel soundtrack (Walt Disney, Leopold Stokowski)
Reverberation in Dead Rooms (Carl Eyring)	1930		
Auralization with scale models (Spandöck)	1933	1944	Portable tape recorders
The Effects of Noise on Man (Karl Kryter)	1950	1948	33-1/3 rpm, 12-inch records (Columbia)
Acoustic computer modeling	1965	1949	45 rpm, 7-inch records (RCA Victor)
PC programs for reverberation time in simple rooms	1981	1953	Ampex two-track tape recorder
Full graphic MacIntosh modeling CAD program (BOSE)	1986	1957	Stereo vinyl standard established
EASE modeling program (Wolfgang Ahnert)	1990	1960	Quadrophonic sound experiments
CATT Acoustics (Beng-Inge Dalenbäck)	1990	1963	The Rolling Stones sign record deal
Concert and Opera Halls (Leo Beranek)	1996	1964	Noise reduction for audio recording (Dolby Labs)
		1966	"Pet Sounds" Beach Boys (Brian Wilson)
		1966	"River Deep Mountain High" Ike and Tina Turner, ("Wall of Sound" by Phil Spector)
		1967	Studer multitrack tape recorder
		1967	"Sergeant Pepper's Lonely Heart's Club Band" The Beatles (George Martin)
		1969	Woodstock Festival
		1970	ARPANET started
		1970	"Earthquake" movie, Sensorround process, large low-frequency horns, vibrations can be felt
		1974	"Tubular Bells" Mike Oldfield, quadraphonic remix released
		1974	Music Television (MTV) introduced
		1980	Compact Disc – Digital Audio
		1982	"Return of the Jedi" movie, introduction of THX sound (George Lucas, Tomlinson Holman)
		1987	5.1 Surround sound format
		1988	IMAX digital sound system introduced (Sonics Associates)
		1989	MP3 patented
		1991	World-Wide Web released (Tim Berners-Lee, CERN)
		1998	Super Audio Compact Disc, DVD-Audio formats
		1999	Napster file sharing application
		2003	Apple iTunes Music Store

ACOUSTICS
The science of sound

AMPLITUDE
The height or magnitude of a pressure wave
at a given time

ATMOSPHERIC PRESSURE
Basic air pressure, depending on
altitude and weather

COMPRESSION
Increase in pressure through the
crowding together of particles

DECIBEL (dB)
1/10 bel. User-friendly unit for sound pressure
level. Named after Alexander Graham Bell

FREQUENCY (f)
Number of cycles per second, in hertz (Hz),
kilohertz (kHz)

FUNDAMENTAL FREQUENCY
The lowest frequency component
of a complex sound

HARMONIC
A sound component of a multiple
of the fundamental frequency

INTERFERENCE
Interaction between different sound waves

LOUDNESS
Subjective perception of a sound pressure level

MEDIUM
Environment through which sound is transmitted

NOISE
Sound with no periodic frequency

OCTAVE
Interval between two sounds with double
or half the frequency or wavelength

PEAK AMPLITUDE
The height, or maximum value of a wave crest

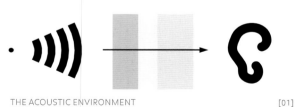

THE ACOUSTIC ENVIRONMENT   [01]

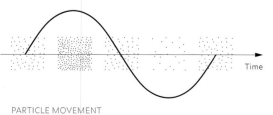

PARTICLE MOVEMENT   [02]

BASIC PHYSICS

THE MULTIPLE NATURE OF ACOUSTICS
The science of sound is connected to, and extends into countless other disciplines. Architectural acoustics, though just a small segment of the entire field, is the focus of most of this book. At its most basic level, two main branches form the foundation of acoustic science:

The first, the fundamental physics of sound, deals with physical events in nature. Sound is propagated through a medium, regardless of human presence. This aspect is outlined very briefly on this chapter.

The second concept concerns the human side of sound; the auditory sensation in the ear, the perception of sound resulting from nerve impulses stimulating the acoustic cortex of the brain. More on this aspect can be found under psycho-acoustics later on.

THE ACOUSTIC ENVIRONMENT
The acoustic environment generally consists of the sound source causing the acoustical vibration, the path of transmission through a medium, and the receiver. All three affect the quality of sound at the receiver.

The source may be desirable sound (e.g. music, speech, ocean waves); or undesirable noise (e.g. traffic, machinery).

The path from source to receiver is influenced by the environmental context and by the nature of the transmission media. [01]

MEDIUM
Particles in a medium, such as air or water, vibrate about their equilibrium positions, receive momentum from collisions, and pass it on to other particles, thus propagating the sound wave.

For sound to be transmitted, a medium must possess both elasticity and inertia. These qualities allow the particles to move, while returning to their original position after the acoustic event is over. [02]

SOUND WAVES
Sound waves are a physical disturbance (vibration) of molecules within a medium.

Water waves are propagated in circular, orbital motions. Light, heat and radio waves are transmitted in transverse motions, with particles vibrating at right angles to the direction of travel.

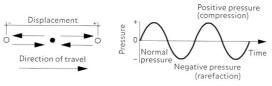

LONGITUDINAL MOTION OF PARTICLES [03]

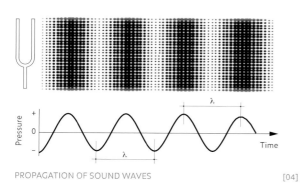

PROPAGATION OF SOUND WAVES [04]

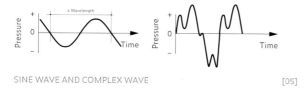

SINE WAVE AND COMPLEX WAVE [05]

APERIODIC SOUND WAVES – NOISE [06]

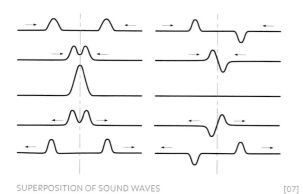

SUPERPOSITION OF SOUND WAVES [07]

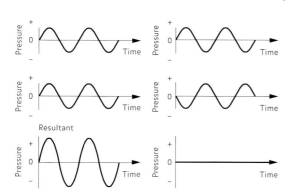

CONSTRUCTIVE AND DESTRUCTIVE INTERFERENCE [08]

Sound waves move through longitudinal motion by the vibration of particles parallel to the direction of travel. [03]

PROPAGATION OF SOUND WAVES
Sound waves are propagated through compression and rarefaction, resulting in microscopic changes in local pressure. These sound pressure vibrations are superimposed on the basic atmospheric pressure. Although each particle only moves very little from its original position, sound waves can travel long distances. [04]

PERIODIC SOUND WAVES
Periodic sound waves are a regularly repeated pattern of oscillation. A sine wave is the simplest form of a periodic wave, representing a pure tone at one single constant frequency. While they do not exist in nature, sine waves can be generated by electronic equipment.

Most periodic waves are more complex combinations of frequencies and pressures over time. [05]

APERIODIC SOUND WAVES – NOISE
Aperiodic sound waves have no periodic frequency or oscillation. They are technically referred to as noise. If the noise is concentrated in a narrow range of frequencies, it is called tonal noise. [06]

WHITE NOISE / PINK NOISE
White noise is random sound with its energy distributed evenly and uniformly throughout the spectrum. Its amplitude is constant across different frequencies, similar to white light. It generally sounds like tape hiss.

Pink noise is also random sound, but with its energy concentrated more in the lower frequencies. It can be compared to red light. *Pink noise* has the same power within each octave. It sounds more pleasant than white noise, like rushing water.

Both are used in the analysis of acoustic environments and equipment.

SUPERPOSITION OF SOUND WAVES
Sound waves traveling in opposite directions can pass through each other and emerge in their original condition. [07]

INTERFERENCE
Two or more waves may support each other through constructive interference, or cancel each other out (destructive interference). A large number of different sound waves traveling in different directions can be superimposed in space, and can still be detected as distinctive from one another. [08]

SPEED OF SOUND
The speed of sound (c) varies greatly according to the elasticity and density of the medium.

The exact speed of sound in air depends on environmental factors such as humidity. Changes in temperature have the greatest effect.

In air at 21 °C (72° Fahrenheit) the speed of sound is approximately 344 meters/second or 1130 feet/second. This is very slow compared to light and radio waves (299,724,000 m/s or 186,000 miles/second).

PERIOD (t)
Time duration of one cycle of vibration,
in seconds (s)

RAREFACTION
Decrease in pressure through spreading
out of particles

RECEIVER
Human listener, microphone, etc.

SOUND
A physical disturbance, such as a vibration or pul-
sation of pressure in an elastic medium

SOUND PRESSURE (p)
Acoustic force per unit area,
in pascals (Pa) 1 Pa = 1 Newton/m^2.

Speed of sound (c) in various materials:

	(m/s)	(f/s)
Rubber	50	164
Air 0 °C	331	1.087
Air 21 °C	344	1.130
Fresh water	1.480	4.856
Salt water	1.520	4.987
Soft wood	3.350	10.991
Hard wood	5.000	16.400
Concrete	3.400	11.155
Steel	5.050	16.568
Aluminum	5.150	16.896
Glass	5.200	17.060
Gypsum board	6.800	22.310

FREQUENCY

Frequency (f) is the rate of pressure changes, vibrations, or wave
cycles occurring during one second, measured in hertz or kilohertz.

Frequency is inversely proportional to the period (t), or duration
of a cycle. The higher the frequency, the shorter the period
of a sound vibration.

$$f = 1 / t \qquad\qquad t = 1 / f$$

Sound is audible to humans within a range of about 20 Hz to 20 kHz.
Frequencies below 20 Hz are called infrasonic and can be sensed as
vibrations. Frequencies above 20 kHz are called ultrasonic. [09]

OCTAVE BANDS AND BANDWIDTH

Series of different frequencies, usually spaced apart by octaves
or fractions thereof, are used to analyze complex sounds. The
bandwidths centered on each frequency vary according to the
spacing of the bands. [10]

SPECTRUM

Sound spectrum graphs can be plotted to represent real-world
sounds, containing a mixture of frequencies and sound pressure levels.
This allows the detailed analysis of complex sound events. [11–12]

DOPPLER EFFECT

In general, the frequency reaching a receiver is the same as the
frequency at the source. But when the source and the receiver
are in motion relative to each other, the perceived sound
frequency changes over time.

This so-called Doppler effect can be observed, for example, when
an ambulance approaches or drives away with its siren sounding.
With decreasing distance, the observed frequency increases;
when moving apart, the observed frequency decreases.

The same phenomenon can be seen in astronomy, where shifts in the
light spectrum help determine the movement of distant stars. [13]

WAVELENGTH

The wavelength (λ) is the distance between two successive peaks of
a sound wave, or the distance a wave travels during one cycle. [14]

A sound's wavelength is inversely proportional to its frequency,
with the speed of sound as a constant:

$$f = c / \lambda \qquad\qquad \lambda = c / f$$

SOUND PRESSURE

Sound pressure (p) is a measure of the acoustic force on a given
area, and represents an increase and decrease above and below
the normal atmospheric pressure.

A change in sound pressure results in a perceived change in
loudness. Human perception ranges from 20 micropascal to
20 pascal (Pa), a ratio of 1 to 1,000,000.

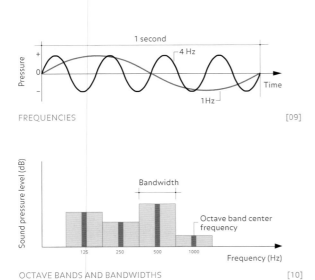

FREQUENCIES [09]

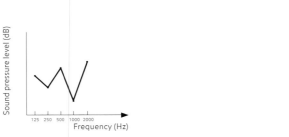

OCTAVE BANDS AND BANDWIDTHS [10]

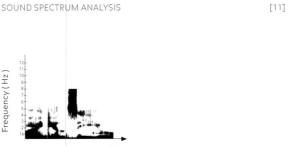

SOUND SPECTRUM ANALYSIS [11]

SOUND SPECTRUM ANALYSIS – SPEECH [12]

DOPPLER EFFECT [13]

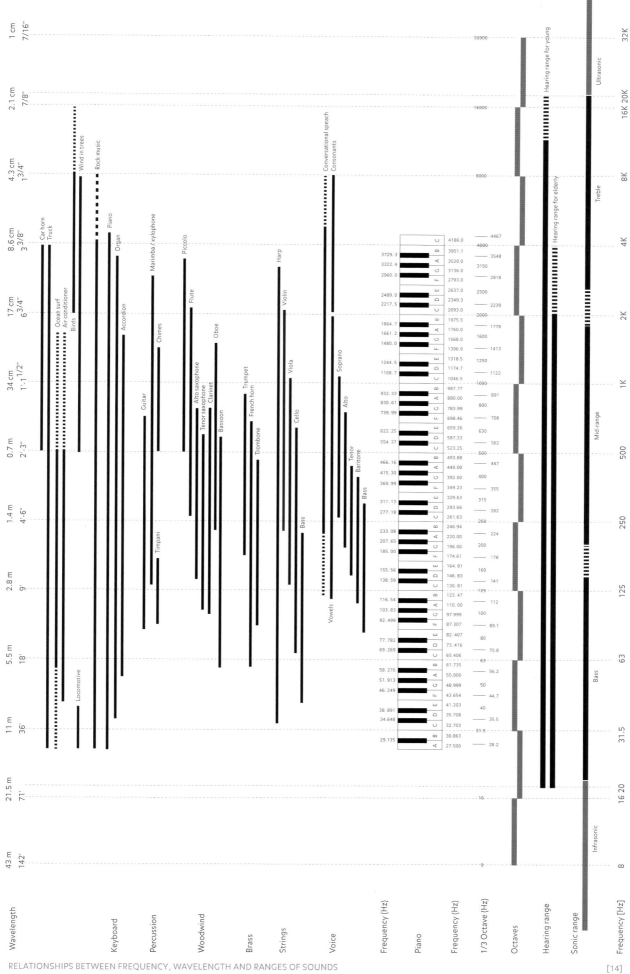

RELATIONSHIPS BETWEEN FREQUENCY, WAVELENGTH AND RANGES OF SOUNDS

SOUND PRESSURE LEVEL (SPL)
Common acoustic measurement, using the
logarithmic decibel (dB) scale

SOUND WAVE
The propagation of sound through compression
and rarefaction in an elastic medium

SOURCE
The originator of a sound vibration

SPECTRUM
Data including frequency, pressure and
level of complex sounds

SPEED OF SOUND (c)
344 m/s; 1130 f/s in air, room temperature

SPHERICAL DIVERGENCE
Spherically spreading of sound from
a point source in free space

TONE
Pure sound, sine wave

WAVELENGTH (λ)
Distance between two peaks of a sound wave,
or distance a wave travels during one cycle

SOUND PRESSURE LEVEL
To compress these large numbers into an easier-to-use format,
sound pressure levels (SPL) are expressed using the logarithmic
decibel (dB) scale.

The range of human hearing extends from the threshold of
hearing, designated as 0 dB to the threshold of pain at 140 dB.

Sound pressure in pascals (Pa) and sound pressure levels in decibels
(dB) are expressions of the same values, and can be converted. [15]

Sound pressure levels of complex sounds vary by individual
frequency, and can be broken down in bands. [17]

CHANGES IN SOUND PRESSURE LEVEL
Because of their logarithmic nature, decibel values cannot be
simply added. To predict changes in sound pressure level when
additional sound sources are added, the following rules of
thumb can be used:

If the difference between two sound levels is:

0–1	dB	add 3 dB to the higher value (e.g. 50dB + 51dB = 54dB)
2–3	dB	add 2 dB to the higher value (e.g. 50dB + 53dB = 55dB)
4–8	dB	add 1 dB to the higher value (e.g. 50dB + 58dB = 59dB)
>8	dB	same as the higher value (e.g. 50dB + 65dB = 65dB)

HUMAN SENSITIVITY TO CHANGES IN SOUND LEVEL
If the difference between two sound levels is:

1	dB	the change in loudness is imperceptible
3	dB	the difference in loudness is barely perceptible
6	dB	there is a clearly noticeable difference in loudness (e.g distance outdoors is halved/doubled)
10	dB	the sound appears about twice (1/2) as loud
20	dB	the sound appears about four times (1/4) as loud

INVERSE SQUARE LAW
The spherical divergence of sound in space determines the decrease
in sound pressure with distance. The inverse square law can be used
to estimate the change in sound pressure level outdoors, in a free-
field condition. It does not apply to reverberant rooms indoors.

It expresses the change in sound pressure level as a function
of varying distances from the source: each doubling of distance
from a point source with spherical sound distribution pattern
translates into a 6 dB loss in sound pressure level. [16]

A line source radiates sound cylindrically and each doubling
of the distance reduces the sound pressure level by only 3 dB.
Examples of line sources are pipes, freeways and trains.

Even less SPL reduction with growing distances occurs if a
sound front emanates from a planar source.

EXAMPLE SOUND SOURCE	SOUND PRESSURE (Pa)	SOUND PRESSURE LEVEL (dB)
Threshold of pain	200.0	140
Jet aircraft engine	20.0	120
Jackhammer	2.0	100
Factory noise	0.2	80
Normal speech	0.02	60
Quiet living room	0.002	40
Quiet recording studio	0.0002	20
Threshold of hearing	0.00002	0

SOUND PRESSURES AND SOUND PRESSURE LEVELS   [15]

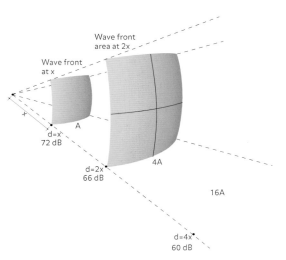

INVERSE SQUARE LAW   [16]

SOURCE	63 Hz	125 Hz	250 Hz	500 Hz	1000 Hz	2000 Hz	4000 Hz	8000 Hz	dBA
RESIDENTIAL INDOORS									
Alarm clock	-	46	48	55	62	62	70	80	80
Electric shaver	59	58	49	62	60	64	60	59	68
Vacuum cleaner	48	66	69	73	79	73	73	72	81
Garbage disposal	64	83	69	56	55	50	50	49	69
Washing machine	59	65	59	59	58	54	50	46	62
Air-conditioning unit	64	64	65	56	53	48	44	37	59
Ringing phone	-	62	44	56	58	73	69	83	83
Stereo loud	60	72	83	82	82	80	75	60	86
Stereo moderate	56	66	75	72	70	66	64	48	75
Violin fortissimo	-	-	91	91	87	83	79	66	92
Normal conversational speech	-	57	62	63	57	48	40	-	63
INTERIORS									
Amplified rock music	116	117	119	116	118	115	109	102	121
Audiovisual room	85	89	92	90	89	87	85	80	94
Auditorium (applause)	60	68	75	79	85	84	75	65	88
Classroom	60	66	72	77	74	68	60	50	78
Computer equipment room	78	75	73	78	80	78	74	70	84
Dog kennel	-	-	90	104	106	101	89	79	108
Gymnasium	72	78	84	89	86	80	72	64	90
Commercial kitchen	86	85	79	78	77	72	65	57	81
Laboratory	65	70	73	75	72	69	65	61	77
Library	60	63	66	67	64	58	50	40	68
Mechanical equipment room	87	86	85	84	83	82	80	78	88
Music practice room	90	94	96	96	96	91	91	90	100
Racquetball court	82	65	80	85	83	75	68	62	86
Reception and lobby area	60	66	72	77	74	68	60	50	78
OUTDOORS									
Birds	-	-	-	-	-	50	52	54	57
Cicadas	-	-	-	-	35	51	54	48	57
Barking dog	-	50	58	68	70	64	52	48	72
Lawn mower	85	87	86	84	81	74	70	72	86
Pistol shot (peak impulse levels)	-	-	-	83	91	99	102	106	106
Surf	71	72	70	71	67	64	58	54	78
Wind in tree leaves	-	-	-	33	35	37	37	35	43
TRAFFIC									
Large truck at 90 km/h	83	85	83	85	81	76	72	65	86
Passenger cars at 90 km/h	72	70	67	66	67	66	59	54	71
Motorcycle at 90 km/h	95	95	91	91	91	87	87	85	95
Snowmobile	65	82	84	75	78	77	79	69	85
Train	95	102	94	90	86	87	83	79	94
Train siren	88	90	110	110	107	100	91	78	109
Car horn	-	-	-	92	95	90	80	60	97
Commercial airplane / 1.5 km from take-off flight path	77	82	82	78	70	56	-	-	78
Helicopter	92	89	83	81	76	72	62	51	80

SOUND PRESSURE LEVEL (dB)

[17]

M. David Egan, *Architectural Acoustics*. McGraw-Hill Publishing Company, New York 1988

AUDITORY CANAL
Ear canal or Meatus; part of outer ear

BASILAR MEMBRANE
Splits the cochlea along its length; seat of the hair cells

BINAURAL
Hearing with two ears

COCHLEA
Spiral organ of the inner ear; transforms
pressure changes into neural impulses

EARDRUM
Tympanum; airtight seal between
outer and middle ear

EUSTACHIAN TUBE
Connects the middle ear to the oral
cavity for pressure equalization

HAIR CELLS
Attached to basilar membrane; transform vibrations
of the basilar membrane into nerve signals

INTERAURAL DIFFERENCE
Time or level difference experienced
between the two ears

(SPATIAL) LOCALIZATION
Determination of the location of a sound source

LOUDNESS (PHONS, SONES)
The perception of sound pressure level

OSSICLES
Hammer, anvil, stirrup; small bones in middle ear

PERCEPTION
Subjective human experience of the
physical aspects of sound

PINNA
External portion of the ear; helps
to capture and localize sound

PITCH (mels)
The perception of frequency

PRECEDENCE EFFECT
Haas effect; helps directional perception
and suppresses early echoes

PSYCHO-ACOUSTICS
Interaction between physics and
the auditory system

THRESHOLD OF HEARING
Lowest perceptible loudness level, 20 mPA at 1 kHz

THRESHOLD OF PAIN (FEELING)
Upper limit of hearing before permanent damage to
ears occurs

TIMBRE
Tone color, harmonic composition of a sound

OUTER EAR   [01]

PSYCHO-ACOUSTICS

HUMAN HEARING
The two main aspects of human hearing are the physiology of the
auditory system, and the processing of sound information in the
brain. The resulting perception of sound is not easily measurable,
and does not always relate to physical events in a linear fashion.

PERCEPTION
Psycho-acoustics is concerned with the perception of sound.
It is not an isolated discipline, but is closely interconnected with
psychology, physiology, biology, medicine, physics, music, engineering, architecture and other fields. The relative and subjective
nature of perception and the complexity of the involved processes are the subjects of much ongoing research.

Human hearing and perception is a complex and highly evolved
system. It can detect a wide range of stimuli and identify them
by pitch, timbre, loudness and location.

PRESSURE RANGE
At the threshold of hearing, the lowest perceptible sound
pressure level, movements of the eardrum can be as small as
one tenth the size of a hydrogen atom. But the ear can also
respond to sound pressures a million times greater, with an
energy content of a trillion (10^{12}) times more.

SELECTIVITY
The auditory system has the ability to select and recognize
different sounds by their frequency and timbre, or to pick
them out of an array of other sounds.

THE PHYSIOLOGY OF HEARING

THE AUDITORY MECHANISM
The ear is divided into three parts: the outer ear, the middle ear
and the inner ear. Each fulfills a distinctive function, from gathering
sound to forwarding information to the central nervous system. [02]

THE OUTER EAR
The pinna, or external ear, reinforces and directs sound into
the ear canal. Its particular shape acts as a comb filter, whose frequency response helps with the localization of sound sources,
especially of higher frequencies. [01]

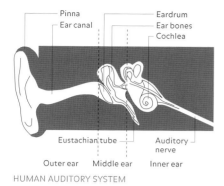

HUMAN AUDITORY SYSTEM [02]

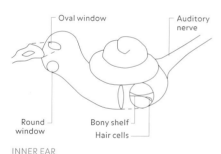

MIDDLE EAR [03]

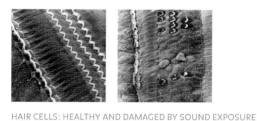

INNER EAR [04]

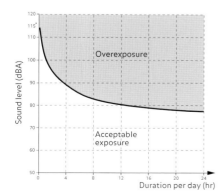

HAIR CELLS: HEALTHY AND DAMAGED BY SOUND EXPOSURE [05]

EXPOSURE TO SOUND [06]

Basically a resonating pipe, the ear canal also reinforces sonic energy. Its resonant frequency lies around 3 kHz, the frequency range to which humans are most sensitive.

THE MIDDLE EAR
The ossicles, three small bones (the hammer, anvil and stirrup) in the middle ear, further reinforce the sound energy arriving at the eardrum. Acting as mechanical levers, they transfer the vibrations to the inner ear. [03]

THE INNER EAR
The fluid-filled and snail-shaped cochlea of the inner ear is the transducer that turns the mechanical energy arriving from the middle ear into electrical signals for the auditory cortex in the brain. Split along its length by the basilar membrane, the cochlea responds to frequency-dependent vibrations, resulting in the perception of pitch. [04]

HEALTH ISSUES
Upper frequency hearing naturally diminishes with age. Long-term, or repeated, exposure to intense sound levels, occupational or recreational, can cause permanent damage at all ages. [05]

Health regulations govern both the loudness level and time of exposure per day. Music industry and medical groups are concerned with the protection of musicians, audio professionals and audiences. [06]

PERCEPTION VERSUS PHYSICS
While measurements of the physical aspects of sound are repeatable and allow an accurate prediction of its variables, human perceptual responses are less predictable.

TERMINOLOGY
Subjective attributes of sound are frequently used to describe sound, especially in music.

PHYSICS	PERCEPTION
Frequency (Hz)	Pitch (mels)
Sound pressure level (dB)	Loudness (phons, sones)
Spectrum	Timbre, or tone color, quality

PITCH
Pitch is the subjective perception of frequency, the characteristic of a sound that makes it sound higher or lower, or that determines its relative position on a scale.

For pure tones, pitch is determined mainly by frequency, but also by sound level. The pitch of complex sounds also depends on the timbre of the sound and its duration.

Absolute pitch is the ability to recognize the pitch of a tone without the use of a reference tone. Less than 0.01 percent of the population have this ability. Most people have a degree of relative pitch recognition, the ability to tell whether a tone is higher or lower than another.

LOUDNESS
The relationship between sound pressure levels and loudness perception is not linear. Equal loudness contours show the average perception of loudness of a large number of test subjects. Sounds with the same perceived loudness level have the same phon value. [07]

The curves indicate that hearing sensitivity diminishes greatly at lower frequencies, and that the greatest sensitivity lies in the area of speech frequencies.

Human hearing occurs between two threshold curves: The threshold of hearing is the minimum audible limit, whereas the threshold of feeling is indicating the beginning of the sensation of pain.

The area of audibility between the two curves includes yet smaller subsets for the ranges of music and speech. [08]

SOUND LEVEL METERING
To measure sound levels for specific applications, weighted curves (A to E) are used. For example A-weighted sound levels (dBA) are adjusted to ignore lower frequencies, much like human hearing. [09]

TIMBRE
Timbre is a subjective quality describing the tonal quality, or tone color of a complex sound. Similar to spectrum in physics, it is a multidimensional attribute of sound, and is often applied to musical instruments.

Timbre has been defined as the attribute of auditory sensation whereby a listener can judge that two sounds are dissimilar using any criteria other than pitch, loudness or duration.

SPATIAL LOCALIZATION
Besides the spectral effect of the pinna, binaural hearing is the main factor in localizing sound sources.

Intensity level differences at the two ears allow localization at higher frequencies. At frequencies below 1.5 kHz, localization is achieved mainly due to interaural time difference between sound paths. [10]

THE PRECEDENCE EFFECT
Also known as the Haas effect, this phenomenon makes it possible to distinguish sounds, even with strong reverberation, by fusing early reflections with the direct sound, resulting in an increase in level.

Direct sound takes precedence over the reverberating echoes within about the first 20 to 40 milliseconds. By emphasizing the direct sound and suppressing reflections, the precedence effect helps with the localization of sound sources.

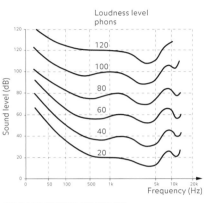

EQUAL LOUDNESS CONTOURS   [07]

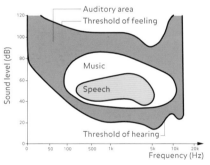

THRESHOLDS AND AUDITORY AREA FOR HUMAN HEARING   [08]

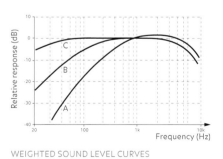

WEIGHTED SOUND LEVEL CURVES   [09]

BINAURAL HEARING   [10]

ENVIRONMENTAL ACOUSTICS

NOISE SOURCES

Environmental acoustics is mainly concerned with noise, or undesirable sounds. Especially in urban conditions, noise levels are increasing with greater population density. Environmental sound levels have increased constantly over time, although complaints about disturbing noise have been commonplace since antiquity.

NATURAL SOUNDS

Naturally occurring sounds are rarely considered bothersome, and are widely accepted as part of the environment. Noise from barking dogs, cowbells, roosters and other animals can sometimes create a disturbance.

MAN-MADE NOISE

Man-made sounds are often disturbing to the public. Music and other noise from groups of people can be perceived as a problem. Growing noise pollution is a regularly raised concern, and is regulated by governmental and private organizations.

TRAFFIC

Street noise from cars, trucks, buses and motorcycles is the most common source of environmental noise. Overall noise levels vary with the number of vehicles, the speed of traffic and road conditions. Engine and exhaust noise is prevalent at lower speeds, tire and wind noise at higher speeds.

Railway noise can emanate from heavy trains or light rail traffic. Subways and surface trains can create vibrations transmitted through earth and structures.

Low-frequency engine noise and whistles and horns from boats can be a problem near waterways.

Aircraft traffic around airports is a large-scale and long-term issue. Although updated airplane designs have led to significant noise reductions, increased air traffic still accounts for much community disturbance. [01]

CONSTRUCTION NOISE

Construction equipment noise can be a great disturbance and, while often temporary, may have to be mitigated.

CONTOUR MAP FOR AIR TRAFFIC NOISE LEVELS   [01]

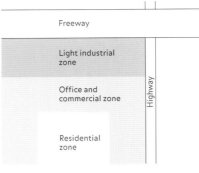

LAND-USE AND ZONING MAPS [02]

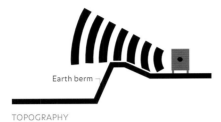

TOPOGRAPHY [03]

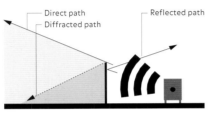

BARRIERS [04]

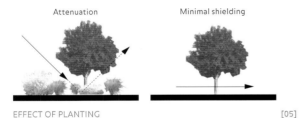

EFFECT OF PLANTING [05]

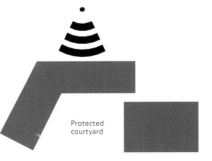

BUILDING ORIENTATION AND SHAPES [06]

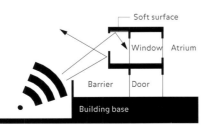

BUILDING FEATURES [07]

MACHINERY
Industrial machinery, as well as cooling, ventilation and electrical equipment can be significant sources of noise in other-wise quiet areas.

SOUND PROPAGATION
Sound is attenuated with increasing distance from a point source, and to a lesser degree from a linear source, such as a freeway. Factors like topography, planting, atmospheric and wind conditions greatly influence propagation.

NOISE SURVEYS
Measurements of noise data can consist of short-term and long-term surveys and when combined, can present a picture of existing or expected noise levels. Besides basic sound level measurements in decibels, recordings can be interpreted through spectrum analyzers for frequency-specific data.

ZONING LAWS
Zoning laws and maps often provide for the separation of quiet and noisy areas. Where inconsistent uses occur (i.e. a recording studio in a residential area, a residential area near a highway) special precautions must be taken. [02]

NOISE MITIGATION MEASURES
Location and relative proximity to potential sound sources is a key factor in determining expected noise levels.

TERRAIN SHAPES
Natural or man-made topographic shapes are very effective in shielding or propagating sound. [03]

OUTDOOR BARRIERS
Freestanding structures and buildings can deflect, absorb or reflect sound, especially higher frequencies. Diffraction around barriers occurs for lower frequencies, making them less effective at greater distances. [04]

VEGETATION
Surface vegetation can help attenuate propagated sound. However, the shielding effect of trees and shrubs is often overestimated. A thin visual barrier of greenery has a negligible effect as a sound barrier. [05]

BUILDING PLACEMENT
The orientation and overall shape of buildings can block or propagate undesired noise and affect sound levels. [06]

BUILDING FEATURES
Barriers, balconies, overhangs, atriums, recesses and surface treatments in building designs can be used to improve acoustical protection from outdoor noise. Shadow zones out of the acoustical line of sight from nearby sources can protect openings. Diffraction around barriers and unwanted reflections from hard surfaces need to be considered.

The correct detailing and construction of building elements like windows, doors and mechanical systems are further steps in blocking unwanted noise. [07]

ROOM ACOUSTICS

Acoustic design is not limited to obvious applications such as concert halls; it is relevant to many other, if maybe more mundane spaces. The prediction and planning of sonic performance is the concern of room acoustics. Like architecture itself, it falls somewhere between the scientific and the intuitive.

Contrary to free-field conditions, the boundaries of a room greatly affect sound in indoor spaces. Most of the sound energy reaching a listener inside a room has already been reflected by surfaces and obstacles.

Sound, with its different frequencies and wavelengths, requires various analytical approaches, depending on its properties. Higher frequencies can be predicted by using ray-acoustic tracing of reflections, similar to light. Lower frequencies are dominated by wave acoustics and normal modes.

GENERAL ROOM PROPERTIES

SIZE
The volume of a room influences its acoustic properties. The sound of large spaces is instinctively understood to be different from smaller rooms.

Small rooms have a tendency towards more pronounced modal resonances related to their specific proportions.

In large rooms, reverberation is more pronounced and echoes are more likely to occur. Long waves have room to develop, and low frequencies respond better.

PROPORTIONS
Room proportions strongly affect acoustic performance, especially in smaller rooms.

Equal (or whole multiples of) room dimensions in different directions result in coinciding resonances. Such problematic proportions reinforce particular standing waves, coloring and distorting bass sounds.

Desirable room proportions, resulting in a favorable even distribution of room modes have been identified by various acousticians. [01–02]

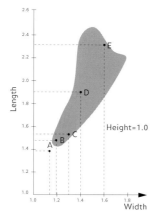

BOLT'S RANGE OF FAVORABLE PROPORTIONS [01]

	LENGTH	WIDTH	HEIGHT	SOURCE
A	1.00	1.14	1.39	Sepmeyer
B	1.00	1.19	1.44	Salter
C	1.00	1.28	1.54	Sepmeyer
D	1.00	1.40	1.90	Louden
E	1.00	1.60	2.33	Sepmeyer

DESIRABLE ROOM PROPORTIONS [02]

ABSORPTION
Transformation of sound energy into heat

ABSORPTION COEFFICIENT (α)
Fraction of sound energy absorbed by a surface

ANECHOIC
Without echoes

ANECHOIC CHAMBER
Room allowing no reflections; for acoustical
testing and measurements

ARTICULATION INDEX (AI)
Rating coefficient for the intelligibility of speech

AXIAL MODE
Most dominant room mode,
between two parallel walls

AURALIZATION
Make audible the acoustics of a room
using scale or computer modeling

COLORATION
Audible acoustic distortion of a signal

DECAY
Decrease of sound energy over time

DIAPHRAGM
Resonant, vibrating panel

DIFFRACTION
Distortion of a wave front caused by an obstacle

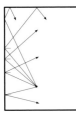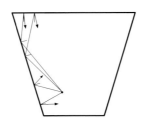

REFLECTION PATTERNS IN DIFFERENT ROOM SHAPES [03]

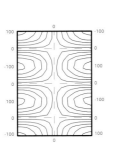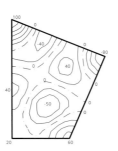

MODAL DISTRIBUTION IN DIFFERENT ROOM SHAPES [04]

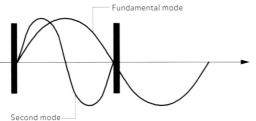

STANDING WAVE [05]

GEOMETRY
Room shapes determine the reflection patterns for high frequencies and the build-up of standing waves for bass frequencies.

Irregularly shaped spaces can permit better design control, but are also more complex to predict. [03–04]

ROOM MODES
Standing waves, or room modes, are due to the build-up of low-frequency sound waves that relate directly to a specific spatial dimension.

The first (fundamental) axial mode between two surfaces occurs when one half of the wavelength corresponds to the room dimension. Harmonic modes occur at multiples of the fundamental frequency. [05]

Additional, weaker standing waves exist: tangential modes between four surfaces, and oblique modes involving six or more surfaces in all three dimensions. [06]

Generally, single dominant room modes are undesirable. They can be minimized by choosing good room proportions and by adding low frequency absorbers. Angling walls and ceilings can improve the distribution of standing waves, but does not eliminate them.

ROOM BOUNDARIES

REFLECTIONS
Flat surfaces, with dimensions sufficiently larger than the wavelength of a sound result in specular reflections, where the angle of reflection equals the angle of incidence. [07]

Reflection patterns depend on the surface shape:

Convex surfaces diffuse wave fronts, creating a wide distribution pattern of the sound energy, and can often be used to acoustical advantage.

Concave surfaces focus wave fronts to one point, creating uneven reflection patterns. Focal points of any geometric form should not be near the location of any receiver.

Corner reflections can be problematic because they reflect sound back in the direction of the incoming wave front. [08]

ECHOES
Distinct echoes are generally undesirable in a space. Concave surfaces can create creep echoes or "whispering galleries".

Flutter echoes can occur in rooms with parallel hard surfaces, or hard concave shapes.

REFLECTION-FREE ZONES
Under certain circumstances, such as in the control room of a recording studio, zones completely free of first order reflections must be created.

DIFFUSION
Diffusion occurs when a wave is reflected from a surface and the sound energy is redistributed diffusely back into the space. To diffuse a sound wave, the reflecting surface should generally have irregularities at approximately the scale of the wavelength of the sound. [09]

To achieve diffusion over a broad band of sound frequencies, all wavelengths must be scattered. Self-similar patterns at different scales, such as fractal geometries, can be layered onto a surface for that purpose. Decorative surfaces and architectural details in historic buildings perform the same function.

Most surfaces reflect sound as a combination of specular and diffuse energy, depending on the frequency range. [10]

Axial   Tangential   Oblique

POSSIBLE ROOM MODES [06]

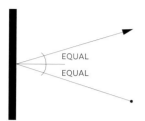

EQUAL
EQUAL

ANGLE OF INCIDENCE = ANGLE OF REFLECTION [07]

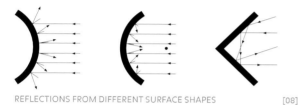

REFLECTIONS FROM DIFFERENT SURFACE SHAPES [08]

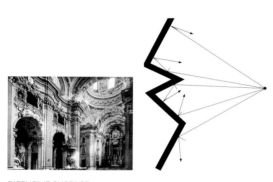

DIFFUSIVE SURFACE [09]
MONASTARY CHAPEL, MELK, AUSTRIA

ENERGY DISTRIBUTION FROM [10]
SPECULAR AND DIFFUSE REFLECTION

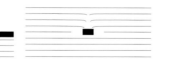

DIFFRACTION [11]

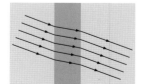

REFRACTION AT CHANGE OF MEDIUM [12]

DIFFUSE SOUND FIELDS
A diffuse sound field is created when the energy from a sound source reaches the listener indirectly, after reflecting off surrounding surfaces, and the sensation of sound coming from all directions at equal levels is achieved.

DIFFRACTION
Sound waves encountering an obstacle can change their direction of travel to bend around it. Similarly, when waves pass through an opening in a surface, they spread out spherically beyond it.

The degree of diffraction depends on the size of the obstacle or opening in relation to the wavelength of the sound. Longer wavelengths diffract more easily; lower frequencies can therefore be heard even when the source is not visible. [11]

REFRACTION
A change in the direction of travel of waves occurs when the speed of propagation changes. This can happen either abruptly at a change of medium in a solid; or gradually, when sound waves travel through air of different temperatures. A similar effect can be experienced in winds of varying speeds. [12–13]

SOUND ABSORPTION
Absorption is the transformation of sound into another form of energy, for example into heat. The level of sound absorption in a space has a great effect on the reverberation time and loudness. Sound absorption is highly frequency dependent.

SOUND ABSORPTION COEFFICIENT
The sound absorption coefficient (α) is the indicator of a material's absorption capacity. It describes the fraction of the incident sound energy a material absorbs at a given frequency.

One square foot of perfect (100%) sound absorption equals 1 sabin.

Materials with a high α (over 0.5) are considered absorptive, materials with a low α (below 0.2) are reflective. [14]

Charts or graphs with the sound absorption coefficients for generic materials across the spectrum are available. Manufacturers provide values for specific building products. [18]

NOISE REDUCTION COEFFICIENT
The NRC is a single number average of a material's absorption coefficients at the middle frequencies. It should only be used for rough estimates.

TOTAL ROOM ABSORPTION
The sum of all room surfaces multiplied by their respective absorption coefficients adds up to the total room absorption.

a = total room absorption (sabin)
S = surface area (sf)(m²)
α = sound absorption coefficient at a given frequency

$$a = \Sigma\,(S \cdot \alpha)$$

ABSORPTION BY AIR
In large spaces, sound absorption by air becomes a significant factor for higher frequencies, resulting in a reduction of sound energy above 1 kHz. [15]

ABSORPTION BY PEOPLE
In spaces with an audience, sound absorption by the occupants is also a factor. Differences between empty and full spaces may be significant. [18]

DIRECT SOUND
Non-reflected sound in the near-field,
directly from the source

DIFFUSION
Scattering or diffuse redistribution
of a sound wave from a surface

ECHO
Delayed reflection perceived as a distinct sound

FLUTTER ECHO
Repetitive echo, usually between
parallel hard surfaces

HELMHOLTZ RESONATORS
Volume resonator; tuned low-frequency
sound absorber

INITIAL TIME DELAY GAP
Time delay between the direct sound
and the first reflection from a surface

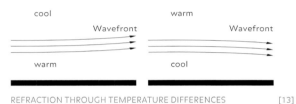

REFRACTION THROUGH TEMPERATURE DIFFERENCES   [13]

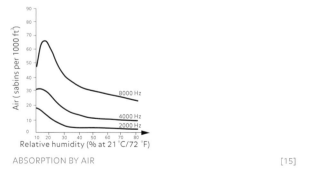

	Opening to free-field	4 cm Fiberglass	Concrete block
Percent reflected	0	20	98
Percent absorbed	100	80	2
Sound absorption coefficient [α]	1.0	0.80	0.02

SOUND ABSORPTION COEFFICIENT α   [14]

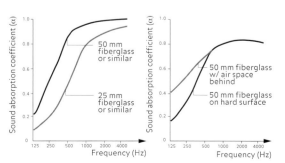

ABSORPTION BY AIR   [15]

POPOUS ABSORBERS – THICKNESS AND AIRSPACE BEHIND   [16–17]

SOUND ABSORPTION METHODS

Three main types of sound absorbers can be differentiated.
The greatest effect across the entire spectrum is achieved with
a combination of different absorbers.

POROUS ABSORBERS

Porous materials, the most commonly used absorbers, include carpet, drapes, "acoustic" ceiling tiles, glass fiber, mineral wool, cotton or felt panels, cellulose, acoustical plaster and open-cell foam.

Porous materials generally absorb mid to high frequencies well.
Absorption occurs through friction in the interstitial spaces within the material. Main factors affecting the absorption are the
thickness, as well as the installation method and, to a lesser
degree, the density of the material. [16–17]

Health concerns about loose fibers in fiberglass have been raised,
and more stable substitutions are available. Newer materials like
cotton, cellulose, foamed and sintered aluminum also offer alternative choices for sound absorption.

Contrary to popular belief, fuzzy, lightweight materials offer almost no insulation value, and have little effect for soundproofing.

BASS TRAPS

So-called bass traps usually consist of porous materials thick
enough to absorb low frequencies. In general, the required
depth, or distance from a wall, of a bass trap is a quarter of the
wavelength to be absorbed. For example, a 32 Hz sound with a
wavelength of 10.5 m (35.5') requires a depth of 2.65 m (8.9').
This is often not a practical solution.

DIAPHRAGMATIC ABSORBERS

Most effective in the low frequency range at their own
resonant frequency, resonating panel absorbers can be tuned
to specific frequencies and wavelengths.

While they can be inadvertently present as glazing, drywall
or paneling, sometimes with adverse effects, they can be used
purposely to supplement porous absorbers, balancing the
overall absorption range.

Diaphragmatic absorbers vibrate in response to sound, thereby
absorbing its energy. Factors affecting the frequency response
are the panel density and the depth of the airspace behind. A
broader bandwidth can be absorbed by adding porous material
inside the airspace, thereby acoustically damping the cavity;
or by varying the depth of the airspace. [19]

VOLUME RESONATORS

Sometimes called Helmholtz resonators, volume absorbers are
useful for narrow-band low frequency absorption. They can be
tuned to a specific frequency.

Factors determining the resonant frequency are the size of
the opening, the depth of the neck and the volume of trapped
air behind it.

The basic concept of a single air-filled bottle in a Helmholtz
resonator can be expanded by combining an array of resonators.
Large surface areas covered with wood strips and slots, or perforated panels can achieve the same effect. Damping the air space,
or varying the depth, result in broader band absorption. [20–21]

Acoustic concrete blocks with cavities and slot patterns are
examples of volume resonators available on the market.

FREQUENCY (Hz)	125	250	500	1000	2000	4000	NRC
FLOORS							
Concrete floor, smooth	0.01	0.01	0.02	0.02	0.03	0.03	0.02
Floor covering: linoleum, cork, rubber, vinyl	0.02	0.03	0.03	0.03	0.03	0.02	0.03
Polished stone, glazed tile	0.01	0.01	0.01	0.01	0.02	0.02	0.01
Wood parquet, glued down	0.04	0.04	0.07	0.06	0.06	0.07	0.06
Wood floor	0.15	0.11	0.10	0.07	0.06	0.07	0.09
Carpet on concrete	0.02	0.06	0.14	0.37	0.60	0.65	0.29
Carpet on soft pad	0.08	0.24	0.57	0.69	0.71	0.73	0.55
WALLS, CEILINGS							
Concrete block raw	0.36	0.44	0.31	0.29	0.39	0.25	0.36
Concrete block painted	0.10	0.05	0.06	0.07	0.09	0.08	0.07
Acoustical concrete block (RPG DiffusorBlox)	0.78	0.90	0.93	0.78	0.80	0.77	0.85
Acoustical concrete block painted (Proudfoot Soundblox)	0.57	0.76	1.09	0.94	0.54	0.59	0.83
Brick raw	0.02	0.03	0.03	0.04	0.05	0.07	0.04
Gypsum board over wood framing, filled with fiberglass	0.55	0.14	0.08	0.04	0.12	0.11	0.10
Plaster on lath	0.14	0.10	0.06	0.05	0.04	0.03	0.06
Plywood panels 3/8"	0.28	0.22	0.17	0.09	0.10	0.11	0.15
Plywood panels 1" over airspace	0.19	0.14	0.09	0.06	0.06	0.05	0.09
Fabric over 1" fiberglass over airspace	0.29	0.82	1.02	1.00	1.03	1.06	0.97
Fabric over 2" fiberglass	0.38	0.60	0.78	0.80	0.78	0.70	0.74
Cotton fiber duct liner 1"	0.07	0.33	0.72	0.99	0.93	0.96	0.74
Cotton fiber insulation 3.5"	0.95	1.30	1.19	1.08	1.02	1.00	1.15
Cotton fiber insulation 5.5"	0.97	1.37	1.23	1.05	1.00	1.01	1.16
Sintered aluminum panels 3mm (Almute) over 2" fiberglass	0.36	0.86	1.13	1.06	0.90	0.71	0.99
Foamed aluminum panels 1" (Alusion)	0.13	0.14	0.55	0.53	0.70	0.85	0.48
Open-cell foam, 1" wedge-shape	0.07	0.11	0.20	0.32	0.60	0.85	0.31
Open-cell foam, 2" wedge-shape	0.08	0.25	0.61	0.92	0.95	0.92	0.68
Wood shredded fiberboard 1" over 1" fiberglass	0.16	0.43	1.00	1.05	0.79	0.98	0.82
Acoustic tile on concrete	0.14	0.20	0.76	0.79	0.58	0.37	0.58
Acoustic tile ceiling 1" suspended	0.76	0.93	0.83	0.99	0.99	0.94	0.94
Glass 1/4" regular window	0.35	0.25	0.18	0.12	0.07	0.04	0.16
Glass heavy laminated	0.18	0.06	0.04	0.03	0.02	0.02	0.04
Drapes light, over flat wall	0.03	0.04	0.11	0.17	0.24	0.35	0.14
Drapes heavy, draped together	0.14	0.35	0.55	0.72	0.70	0.65	0.58
LOW-FREQUENCY ABSORBERS (EXAMPLES)							
Resonant panel absorber 10mm	0.28	0.22	0.17	0.09	0.10	0.11	
Volume absorber 4mm panel, 100mm air with 50mm fiberglass, 1.4% opening	0.25	0.96	0.66	0.26	0.16	0.10	
SOUND ABSORPTION BY AUDIENCE							
Occupied seats	0.60	0.74	0.88	0.96	0.93	0.85	0.88
Unoccupied leather seats	0.44	0.54	0.60	0.62	0.58	0.50	0.59

SOUND ABSORPTION COEFFICIENTS (α)   [18]

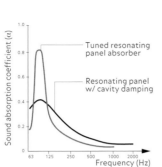

DIAPHRAGMATIC ABSORBERS   [19]

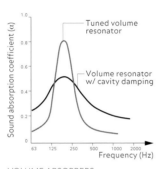

VOLUME ABSORBERS   [20]

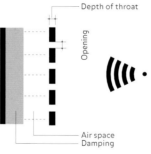

VOLUME ABSORBER DETAIL   [21]

	NC OR RC (N) RANGE
EXCELLENT, CRITICAL LISTENING CONDITIONS	< NC-20
Concert halls, recording studios, etc.	
GOOD LISTENING CONDITIONS	NC-20 to NC-30
Auditoriums, theaters, meeting rooms,	
executive offices, conference rooms, etc.	
QUIET ROOMS	NC-25 to NC-35
Bedrooms, residences, hotels, hospitals	
Offices, classrooms, libraries	NC-30 to NC-35
Large offices, reception areas, stores,	
restaurants, gymnasiums	NC-35 to NC-40
Lobbies, laboratories, maintenance areas	NC-40 to NC-45
Kitchens, laundries, shops	NC-45 to NC-55

PREFERRED RANGE OF NOISE CRITERIA   [22]

ACOUSTIC DESIGN

The relatively low speed of sound is one of the reasons for acoustical problems in rooms. We can easily perceive differences in the arrival time of direct and reflected sounds. Echoes and re-verberations are serious defects in many rooms. Other concerns are noise reduction, speech intelligibility and background noise levels.

NOISE CRITERIA
Noise criteria curves are used to describe the level of desired or acceptable background noise in a room, either to evaluate an existing situation, or to specify a design value. [22]

NC curves compensate for the lower sensitivity of the ear at lower frequencies. [23]

REVERBERATION
Addressing the build-up and decay of sound over time, reverber-ation has been one of the most important aspects of room acous-tics. While other relevant research has been added constantly since the early days, reverberation still remains important. Rever-beration times that are too long make speech perception difficult or impossible. If reverberation is too short, rooms sound "dead", and sound propagation is limited.

REVERBERATION TIME
Reverberation time is the duration it takes for the sound in a room to decay by 60 dB (also RT-60), or for a very loud sound to become effectively inaudible. [24]

Sabine's formula is used to predict reverberation time:

$$T = 0.161 \cdot V/a \qquad \text{(metric)}$$
$$T = 0.049 \cdot V/a \qquad \text{(in feet)}$$

T = reverberation time (time required for a sound to decay 60 dB after the sound has stopped) in seconds.
V = room volume in cubic meters (m³) or cubic feet (ft³)
a = total room absorption in sabins = $\Sigma (S \cdot \alpha)$

or:

$$T = 0.161 \cdot V/(S_1\alpha_1 + S_2\alpha_2 + S_3\alpha_3 + ... S_n\alpha_n) \quad \text{(metric)}$$
$$T = 0.049 \cdot V/(S_1\alpha_1 + S_2\alpha_2 + S_3\alpha_3 + ... S_n\alpha_n) \quad \text{(in feet)}$$

This formula is accurate for most general acoustic calculations in relatively diffuse conditions, and with "normal" proportions, at about 500 Hz. For stricter requirements, more precise methods are available.

Reverberation is directly related to room volume; a greater room volume results in proportionally more reverberation.

Reverberation is inversely proportional to the amount of sound absorbing material in a space. More absorbing material results in less reverberation.

Reverberation time is frequency-dependent and needs to be checked for each octave band. Three-dimensional illustrations called "waterfall graphs" show reverberant decay as a function of frequency and time. [25]

Different room uses require different reverberation times. [26]

NOISE REDUCTION
Sound levels in a room build up due to reflections from its enclos-ing surfaces. The size of the room and the amount of absorption in it determine the build-up of sound levels.

Noise reduction due to the addition or removal of absorbing ma-terial can be predicted. Since absorption varies with frequency, calculations should be made for all frequencies where absorption coefficients are known.

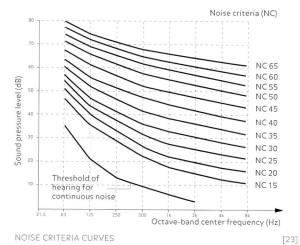

NOISE CRITERIA CURVES [23]

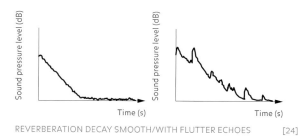

REVERBERATION DECAY SMOOTH/WITH FLUTTER ECHOES [24]

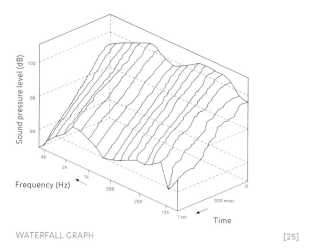

WATERFALL GRAPH [25]

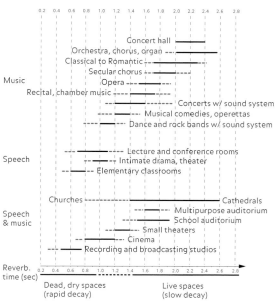

DESIRABLE REVERBERATION TIMES [26]

NR is the reduction of reverberant noise; it does not apply near a source where direct sound is prevalent.

ROOMS FOR SPEECH

A high level of speech intelligibility is the main goal in rooms such as classrooms, auditoriums, drama theaters, meeting rooms, courtrooms, etc. Factors affecting intelligibility are the source level, background noise and reverberation. Low signal-to-noise ratios, especially in the frequency range of speech, make it difficult for listeners to understand a speaker. Noise criteria (NC) provide guidelines for acceptable background noise levels.

Long reverberation times interfere with speech intelligibility. Besides room acoustic treatments, such as aimed reflectors and absorptive surfaces, provisions for electronic amplification of speech are often made.

ROOMS FOR MUSIC

The subject of spaces for live music performance has filled volumes, and is considered the epitome of room acoustics.

Objective values and parameters for acoustic performance exist. Ongoing research continually adds new insights and increased knowledge, and growing computing power aid in the design and evaluation. However, more elusive and intuitive aspects are still part of the design process. The subjective impression of an audience is still the ultimate measure of a successful project.

The reverberation time, loudness, early-to-late sound ratio and the initial time gap can be measured objectively. Other measures exist and more are being developed in an effort to quantify more of the factors contributing to good sound.

Terms like intimacy, clarity, spaciousness, warmth, liveness, balance and blend are used to describe the subjective attributes of a space.

Even spaces for classical music are increasingly being supplemented with active acoustic devices, often without the awareness of the audience.

In rooms used mainly for amplified music, the requirements differ from purely acoustical rooms. The design of the room itself is supplemented or even replaced by the sound system.

OFFICES

In the office workplace, speech privacy is a major concern. Sufficient sound insulation ratings and detailing for walls and ceilings, and the control of flanking paths are needed for closed offices. In open-plan office areas, absorptive surfaces and partitions help to provide privacy.

MULTIPURPOSE ROOMS

Rooms that serve various purposes, such as speech and music, pose acoustic challenges. Sonic properties averaging the optimum conditions for each use are often designed, yielding satisfactory results. For stricter demands, variable or active acoustic methods can be employed.

VARIABLE ACOUSTICS

Acoustic conditions in a space can be varied through many different means. Methods can range from pulling a curtain over a hard surface to a completely computer-controlled adjustable environment.

Contemporary concert halls may feature complex moving canopies or shutters, which can vary the air volume in a space, as well as the geometry, and the level of absorption, reflection and diffusion. Low-tech versions of the same concepts have long been utilized in studios and performance spaces.

The practicality, ease of use and the added time for users to rehearse and get acquainted with a room are important issues to consider. [27]

NOISE CRITERIA (NC)
Single number value for the noise level

NOISE REDUCTION COEFFICIENT (NRC)
Single number average of a material's
absorption properties

POROUS ABSORBERS
Soft, fuzzy materials with small interstitial spaces

RAY ACOUSTICS
Geometric tracing of high-frequency ray patterns

REFLECTION
Change in the direction
of a sound wave at a surface

REFRACTION
Change in the direction of wave travel
at a change of medium

RESONANCE
Vibration occurring at the natural
frequency of a system

REVERBERATION
Decay of sound within an enclosure, depending
on reflections from the room boundaries

REVERBERATION TIME (RT/RT-60)
Time it takes for a sound to decay by 60 dB

ROOM ACOUSTICS
Concerned with sound within an enclosure

ROOM MODES
Modal resonances in a space

STANDING WAVES
A stable wave condition caused
by modal resonances

WAVE ACOUSTICS
Behavior of lower sound frequencies

VARIABLE ACOUSTIC ELEMENTS   [27]
CONCERT HALL LUCERNE, SWITZERLAND

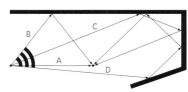

RAY-TRACING   [28]

ACTIVE ACOUSTICS
Electronic sound masking systems are sometimes used in office environments to provide an artificial background noise level and to improve speech privacy where ambient noise levels are too low.

Active noise reduction through electronics is a developing field. Through the recording and simultaneous playback with opposite phase of the ambient noise, the sound energy is cancelled. Currently feasible only for simple problems like fan noise in air conditioning ducts, development of active noise reduction is under way for larger applications.

Amplification and the enhancement of natural acoustics with electronic means are now gaining ground even in the field of classical music. Reverberation level and other factors can be manipulated through electronic processors, using microphones and loudspeakers. These methods can be useful in multipurpose rooms, to adjust them to precise demands. Although good results can be achieved, the basic premise remains controversial for many.

ACOUSTIC SIMULATION METHODS
Audio demonstrations can recreate acoustic events virtually in a neutral environment. This allows the presentation to an audience and the prediction of existing and future conditions.

ROOM ACOUSTIC SIMULATIONS
The prediction of room-acoustic performance is an important tool for the design of spaces for sound. Much progress has been made since Wallace Sabine's development of calculation methods for reverberation times over a century ago. Increasing computing power and ongoing research allow as yet unbuilt spaces to be modeled and auralized. Despite impressive advances, the precise and complete prediction of sonic performance remains elusive and is as much an art as a science.

DRAWINGS
Simple room acoustic analysis can be performed with two-dimensional drawings. Ray-tracing of sound paths is possible for high-frequency sounds, but useless for lower frequencies. Limited results can be achieved for isolated aspects of room acoustics. [28]

CALCULATIONS
Mathematical calculations and numerical analysis of data are the basis for establishing critical wavelengths, low frequency response and room modes, as well as all other acoustical properties.

Reverberation time calculations are a common tool for basic acoustic information.

PHYSICAL ARCHITECTURAL MODELS
Architectural models for acoustic testing were the closest approximation of anticipated performance before the development of advanced computer modeling. They are still employed for large-scale projects and to verify the computer data.

Airtight models, filled with gas to account for the change in scale, can be used to perform three-dimensional tests. The frequencies of the test sounds are adjusted to the scale of the model. Dummies, with hollow chest cavities, clothes and hair to simulate the audience, are equipped with moveable microphones to test each seat individually with frequency scaled sound sources placed on the stage. [29]

COMPUTER MODELS
Modeling programs of varying complexity are available for acoustic predictions. [30]

Analysis programs for basic information on rectangular rooms are available at a relatively low cost. [31]

Proprietary programs for complex spaces have been developed by consulting firms for their own use; others are commercially available to the public.

ACOUSTIC MODEL [29]
DISNEY CONCERT HALL LOS ANGELES, USA

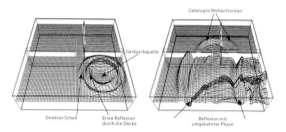

ACOUSTICAL COMPUTER MODEL [30]

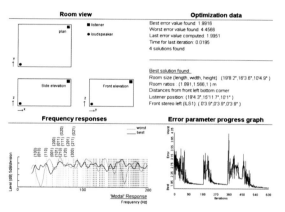

ACOUSTICAL DATA FOR RECTANGULAR SPACES [31]
(ROOM SIZER, RPG)

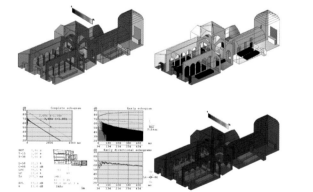

COMPLEX MODELING AND AURALIZATION [32]
(CATT-ACOUSTIC)

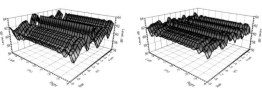

SHAPE-OPTIMIZATION (RPG) [33]

Common to all is the basic process of modeling the space, with acoustical properties assigned to each surface element. Using advanced digital signal processing, the computer plots sound paths and reflections, and creates a mathematical model of the distributed sound energy.

AURALIZATION
Besides visual information and numeric data, advanced programs can simulate acoustical performance and present it in audio formats. The output can be heard on binaural headphones or in specialized rooms with speaker arrays. The virtual models of the acoustic environment can be used to present information for any location within a space. With increasing computing power and speed, real-time modeling of virtual acoustic events, while moving through a virtual space, is becoming a reality. [32]

SHAPE OPTIMIZATION
In a further development of acoustic modeling, new programs allow for the direct shaping of surfaces as a result of acoustic demands. Not just evaluating the pre-determined designs, but actively forming the results, these systems aim to make acoustic treatment an integral part of architectural design. [33]

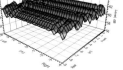

AIRBORNE SOUND
Sound transmitted through air

BARRIER, PANEL, PARTITION
A wall, ceiling, floor, window, door or other
building element considered part of the
insulation assembly

COINCIDENCE DIP
Loss of insulation value at a panel's
resonant frequency

FLANKING PATHS
Secondary paths of sound transmission

IMPACT INSULATION (Isolation) CLASS (IIC)
Rating of a floor or ceiling
for blocking impact sound

LEAKAGE
Loss of insulation value through
a small opening in a partition

MASS
Weight, density of a material

NOISE
Undesirable sound, to be kept away

SOUND INSULATION
Soundproofing; reduction of sound
transmission through a barrier

SOUND TRANSMISSION CLASS (STC)
Rating of a partition for blocking airborne sound

SOUND TRANSMISSION LOSS (TL)
Sound reduction value of a partition
expressed in decibels

SOUND TREATMENT
Interior measures to control the acoustic
properties of a space within that space

STRUCTURE-BORNE SOUND
Sound transmitted through a solid,
usually part of a building

VIBRATION
Structure-borne transmission of sound,
usually at lower frequencies

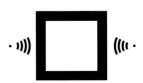

BASIC SOUND INSULATION PROBLEMS   [01]

SOUND INSULATION

PROBLEM DEFINITION
Acoustical issues are often fundamentally misunderstood, even
by those familiar with architectural planning and the general behavior of sound. The lack of a clear problem definition can contribute to, or even be the source of serious difficulties in finding
the appropriate solution.

The two main areas to be distinguished within architectural
acoustics are sound insulation (soundproofing) and acoustic
room treatment (room acoustics). Establishing the nature of
the acoustic problem is the first step to its elimination.

While room acoustics deals with sound within a space, sound
insulation is concerned with sound entering or emanating
from space. [01]

SOUND INSULATION

Soundproofing is one of the very basic problems in acoustic construction. Reducing the transmission of sound from one area to another, usually through a solid barrier, is a common requirement.

Sound transmission works both ways: sometimes sound needs
to be prevented from escaping a room, sometimes from entering
it. Often, both are mutually required.

The degree and type of needed insulation can vary widely
and has to be evaluated and established to avoid insufficient,
misguided or excessive construction measures.

BASIC METHODS OF ACOUSTIC SEPARATION
A few basic strategies can be used to achieve the desired
sonic separation:

LOCATE CRITICAL AREAS AWAY FROM EACH OTHER
While often not feasible due to external factors, such as the
available space, choosing optimum adjacencies can significantly
reduce the need for sound insulating construction. Distance is a
major factor in reducing sound energy, particularly for airborne
sound. Attention must be paid to all three spatial directions, e.g.
horizontal separation in a building can be rendered
meaningless by a close vertical adjacency. [02]

REDUCTION THROUGH SPATIAL SEPARATION [02]

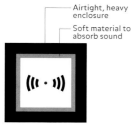

Airtight, heavy enclosure
Soft material to absorb sound

REDUCTION AT THE SOURCE [03]

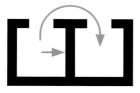

FLANKING PATH [04]

Noleak
TL 40 dB

Airleak
TL 30 dB

Noleak
TL 75 dB

Airleak
TL 30 dB

EFFECT OF LEAKAGE [05]

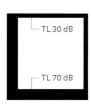

TL 30 dB

TL 70 dB

Overall
TL 30 dB

EFFECT OF INCONSISTENT CONSTRUCTION [06]

REDUCE THE NOISE AT THE SOURCE
The reduction of the sound energy at the source is a very effective way of reducing sound transmission. Where possible, this method can produce good results at minimum cost. [03]

REDUCE THE NOISE AT THE RECEIVING LOCATION
This is not as effective as reducing the source level, but modest improvements can be achieved by adding sound absorption to the receiving room. Technically more a room acoustic strategy, this method can reduce the effect of transmitted sound, although at the expense of the sonic characteristics within the space.

BLOCK THE PATH FROM THE SOURCE TO THE CRITICAL SPACE
The main subject of this chapter, sound insulation through construction elements is the most common method of reducing sound transmission in buildings.

TYPES OF SOUND TRANSMISSION

Sound transmission occurs through the interaction between sound in air and sound in solids. The two basic types of sound transmission in buildings are airborne and structure-borne sound. Although one or the other is usually predominant, a combination of both is common, and they should both be evaluated in parallel for comprehensive results.

AIRBORNE SOUND
Sound waves transmitted through the medium of air. The best defense against airborne sound is an airtight enclosure.

Sound waves resonate a panel (e.g. a wall) – the vibrating panel re-radiates sound, acting as a new, but weaker sound source. The reduction of the sound energy is achieved by dissipation into the structure or reflection of the energy back to the source.

STRUCTURE-BORNE SOUND
Sound waves transmitted through solids, such as floors, walls, ceilings. Typical examples of structure-borne sound are footfall and vibrations caused by machinery.

FACTORS COMPROMISING SOUND INSULATION

FLANKING PATHS
Sound, like water, will find the path of least resistance. Flanking paths around sound insulating elements can severely compromise the whole system. Secondary sound paths can easily be over-looked, but should be avoided. [04]

LEAKAGE
Even small breaks in an assembly reduce the effect of sound insulation measures significantly. A hole only one ten-thousandths of the total enclosure area can decrease the overall sound transmission value to half or less. The higher the basic insulation value is without an air leak, the greater the detrimental effect of any break. [05]

WEAK LINKS
The weakest link in any construction assembly will have the greatest impact on the overall level of sound insulation. A solid wall is only as soundproof as the window, the door, or the airduct opening cut in-to it.

INCONSISTENCY
Most problems with insulation assemblies are due to inconsistencies in the design approach or construction. Comprehensive planning and evaluating of all possible ways of transmission is essential. [06]

SOUND TRANSMISSION LOSS (TL)
The reduction of sound energy between spaces is called Sound Transmission Loss (TL). The desired difference between the noise level on one side (source) and the noise level on the other (receiver) determines the required TL value of the structure. A greater transmission loss value indicates better sound insulation. [07]

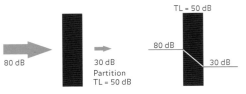

SOUND TRANSMISSION LOSS   [07]

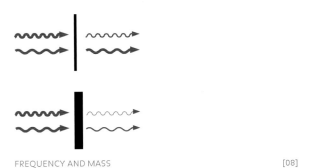

FREQUENCY AND MASS   [08]

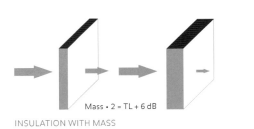

Mass · 2 = TL + 6 dB

INSULATION WITH MASS   [09]

COINCIDENCE DIP   [10]

DUAL PANELS WITH EQUAL TOTAL MASS   [11]

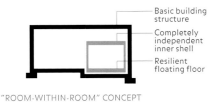

Basic building structure
Completely independent inner shell
Resilient floating floor

"ROOM-WITHIN-ROOM" CONCEPT   [12]

INSULATION METHODS

Successful ways to increase the transmission loss values of a structure include the use of heavy mass, composite construction systems, structural separations, separation with airspace. Most effective are combinations of any of the above.

INSULATION WITH MASS
- Heavyweight construction generally achieves better sound insulation values than lightweight construction.
- The insulation value of a barrier is also related to the frequency or wavelength of the sound.
- Higher frequencies require more force to vibrate a barrier – lower frequencies are transmitted with less force.
- A heavy barrier requires more force to vibrate – a lightweight panel vibrates more easily.
- Barriers with little mass offer limited transmission loss values; even less for lower frequencies than for higher frequencies.
- Barriers with heavy mass result in high transmission loss values, especially for high frequencies. [08]

MASS LAW THEORY
For homogenous building materials every doubling of the mass adds about 6 dB of transmission loss at a given frequency. [09]

For homogenous building materials every doubling of the transmitted frequency increases the transmission loss by about 6 dB, or the STC value by about 5 dB.

A panel generally has a greater insulation value at high frequencies than at low frequencies.

COINCIDENCE DIPS
The inherent resonant frequency of a material or assembly results in a reduced insulation value at that particular frequency. [10]

Materials with the same mass can have varying resonant frequencies due to the different rigidity of different materials or method of attachment and assembly.

DUAL PANEL AND COMPOSITE PARTITIONS
Improvements over homogenous constructions can be achieved by dividing the same total mass into multiple layers, or by composite constructions of varying materials.

Coupling by rigid connections between layers reduces the effect of multiple panels. Coupling through airspace can be reduced by controlling the reverberant sound in the cavity with sound absorbing material.

Composite constructions with varying resonant frequencies for different layers increase sound insulation. [11]

INSULATION THROUGH STRUCTURAL SEPARATION
Although sometimes difficult and almost always expensive to achieve, a significant increase in transmission loss is made possible by structural separation. The total insulation value is greater with equal mass if the structure is separated and has none or few rigid connections.

Typical examples of separated constructions are floating floors and multiple shell floating "room-within-room" constructions. [12]

COMBINATIONS
For high levels of sound insulation, both high mass and structural separation are required. The most effective sound-insulating enclosures are heavy, made of several composite layers, are structurally separated and airtight.

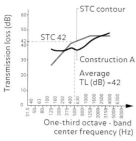

SOUND TRANSMISSION CLASS [13]

STC - SOUND TRANSMISSION CLASS

For purposes of comparison and evaluation it is often desirable to provide a single-number rating of the transmission loss of a barrier for airborne sound.

After sampling the TL of a panel at different frequencies, the results can be compared to a standard STC curve. The resulting number, based on the performance at a frequency of 500 Hz, is the STC (Sound Transmission Class) rating of the partition. [13–14]

IMPACT NOISE

Impact noise is transmitted as structure-borne sound before being radiated into the air at the receiving end. Footsteps on hard floors can be mitigated through the addition of a soft surface, such as carpet. Impact vibrations from equipment can be reduced by the separation of the source from the structure with resilient supports. [15]

IIC – IMPACT INSULATION CLASS

Sampling of the audible sound level through a partition results in values at various frequencies. A standardized impact noise generator is used to produce the noise. Comparison with a standard contour gives a single IIC (Impact Insulation Class) rating for the assembly. [16]

BUILDING VIBRATION

Structure-borne vibrations can be perceived directly by people, either as an audible or a physical whole body sensation. Frequencies above 100 Hz are typically heard as sound, while frequencies below 20 Hz can typically be felt as physical vibrations. In between, combinations of heard and felt sensations are common.

Vibrations can also have an adverse effect on sensitive equipment, e.g. in laboratories, medical facilities and manufacturing plants.

STEADY STATE VIBRATIONS

Mechanical equipment noise is the most common generator of steady state vibrations.

RANDOM VIBRATIONS

Footfall from people walking or running, usually on a floor above, is an example of intermittent, random vibration. Floors are the most common building elements to receive these impacts.

Vibrations through the soil from trains, subways or freeways can also be a source of concern.

VIBRATION CONTROL

The most effective method of vibration control is to limit impact at the source. Once structure-borne vibrations are present, most structures transmit them easily throughout buildings. Isolation efforts at the receiving end are usually much less successful.

To interrupt the path of vibrations in buildings, flexible suspensions and supports, resilient construction methods and floating construction methods are necessary.

	125	250	500	1000	2000	4000	STC
WALL 2x4 wood studs with 1/2" gypsum board both sides, filled with fiber- glass insulation	15	30	34	44	46	41	37 dB
WALL 6" solid concrete with 1/2" plaster both sides	39	42	50	58	64	67	53 dB
DOOR 1-3/4" hollow core wood, No gaskets, air gap	14	19	23	18	17	21	19 dB
DOOR 1-3/4" hollow core steel, filled with fiberglass insulation, gaskets and drop seal	23	28	36	41	39	44	38 dB
GLASS 1/8" float glass	18	21	26	31	33	22	26 dB
GLASS 1/4" laminated, + 3/16" solid, with 4" air space	36	37	48	51	50	58	48 dB

SOUND TRANSMISSION CLASS RATINGS [14]

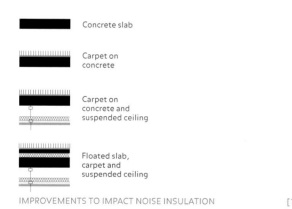

Concrete slab

Carpet on concrete

Carpet on concrete and suspended ceiling

Floated slab, carpet and suspended ceiling

IMPROVEMENTS TO IMPACT NOISE INSULATION [15]

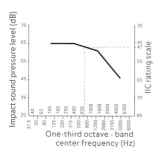

IMPACT INSULATION CLASS RATING [16]

MECHANICAL AND ELECTRICAL SYSTEMS

GENERAL ISSUES
Building systems, such as mechanical, electrical and plumbing equipment can have a significant impact on the acoustic perform-ance of a building. Noise and vibration may be generated by the equipment itself, and ducting and piping can result in the trans-mission of sound from one part of a building to another.

BASIC PLANNING
Acoustical aspects should be considered in the early stages of the engineering process for building systems. Careful planning of adjacencies and layout options can improve and facilitate the final performance and is the most cost-effective form of noise control.

Sound-generating and sound-sensitive spaces should be located apart, with sufficient distances and buffer zones between them. Both horizontal and vertical adjacencies need to be considered. Sufficient space for equipment, clearances and access should be provided early on.

ESTABLISHING CRITERIA
Establishing noise criteria (NC) or room criteria (RC) for each space helps to determine appropriate layouts and connections. In addition to the basic NC ratings, RC levels provide data on the frequency content of noise:

RC(N)   neutral room criteria
RC(R)   rumbly room criteria (with excessive bass frequencies)
RC(H)   hissy room criteria (with excessive treble frequencies)

NOISE CONTROL
Specific noise and vibration control measures for equipment rooms and distributed equipment can include room enclosures, equip-ment mounting systems, vibration isolation hangers and more.

HEATING, VENTILATION, AIR CONDITIONING
Air distribution ducting may compromise sound insulation ef-forts, and is a major source of problems in sound sensitive struc-tures.

DUCTS
Larger ducts result in lower airspeeds, and less air flow noise. But larger cross sections increase penetration sizes through partitions, and reduce insulation values. Sound travels more easily within wider ducts.

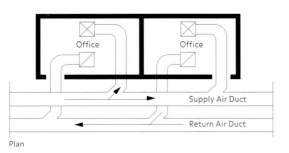

Air duct

Office   Office

Section
CROSS-TALK   [01]

Office   Office

Supply Air Duct

Return Air Duct

Plan
BETTER DUCT LAYOUT   [02]

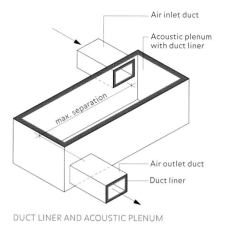

DUCT LINER AND ACOUSTIC PLENUM　　　　　　[03]

Air inlet duct
Acoustic plenum
with duct liner
max. separation
Air outlet duct
Duct liner

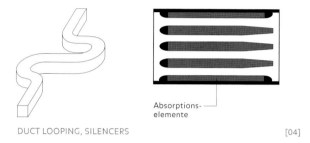

Absorptions-
elemente

DUCT LOOPING, SILENCERS　　　　　　　　　　[04]

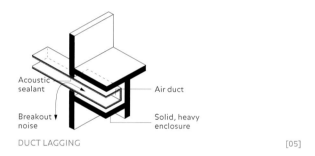

Acoustic
sealant
Air duct
Breakout
noise
Solid, heavy
enclosure

DUCT LAGGING　　　　　　　　　　　　　　　[05]

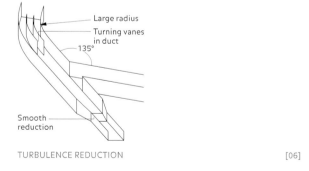

Large radius
Turning vanes
in duct
135°
Smooth
reduction

TURBULENCE REDUCTION　　　　　　　　　　[06]

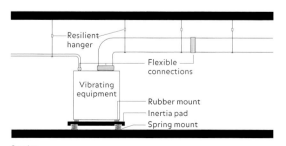

Resilient
hanger
Flexible
connections
Vibrating
equipment
Rubber mount
Inertia pad
Spring mount

Section

FLEXIBLE EQUIPMENT CONNECTIONS　　　　　　[7]

AIR SPEEDS AT OUTLETS

		(ft/s)	(m/s)
Recording studio	RC(N) <20	5.0	1.5
Conference room	RC(N) 25–30	6.5	2.0
Closed office	RC(N) 30–35	8.0	2.5
Open office area	RC(N) 35–45	10.0	3.0

DUCT LAYOUT
Cross talk between spaces occurs when the distance between outlets is short. [01–02]

NOISE TRANSMISSION THROUGH DUCTS
Transmission of equipment noise and cross-talk can be reduced by increasing airflow distances or adding sound-absorbing duct liner, acoustical plenums or silencers. [03–04]

PARTITION PENETRATIONS
Duct and pipe penetrations through walls should be sealed to prevent leaks. Fluid-carrying pipes should not be in rigid contact with partitions, otherwise they will reinforce and radiate the pipe noise.

BREAK-OUT NOISE
Noise escaping through vibrating duct walls is often referred to as break-out noise. It can be reduced by encasing the duct in gypsum board or duct-lagging material like heavy vinyl sheets. [05]

AIR TURBULENCE
Noise from airflow is minimized if turbulence is eliminated as far as possible. Smooth transitions, rounded turns with large radius, turning vanes and Y-shaped take-offs reduce turbulence. The selection of quiet grilles and registers is also critical. [06]

EQUIPMENT MOUNTING
Room enclosures can take care of airborne equipment noise. To prevent structure-borne vibrations to the building, resilient mounting of equipment is necessary. "Floating" floors, resilient spring or rubber mounts, or even inertia pads are often required. [07]

PIPE, DUCT MOUNTING
Transmission of vibrations from equipment to the structure can also occur through connecting pipes and ducts. The use of isolation hangers and mounts and flexible connectors to equipment prevents short-circuiting of the equipment mounting.

SOURCES
– Charles M. Salter Inc., *Acoustics – Architecture, Engineering, the Environment*, San Francisco, Charles M. Salter Inc., 1998
– M. David Egan, *Architectural Acoustics*, McGraw-Hill, Inc., 1988
– Christoph Zürcher, Thomas Frank, *Bauphysik – Bau und Energie*, vdf Hochschulverlag AG, ETH Zurich and B.G. Teubner, Stuttgart, 1998
– Leo Beranek, *Concert and Opera Halls – how they sound*, Acoustical Society of America, 1996
– Glen Ballou, editor, *Handbook for Sound Engineers – The New Audio Cyclopedia*, Howard W. Sams & Co., 1987
– F. Alton Everest, *Master Handbook of Acoustics*, Fourth Edition, The McGraw-Hill Companies, Inc., 2001
– Gottfried C. O. Lohmeyer, *Praktische Bauphysik*, Fourth Edition, B.G. Teubner Stuttgart/Leipzig/Wiesbaden, 2001
– Thomas D. Rossing, *The Science of Sound*, Second Edition, Addison-Wesley Publishing Company, Inc., 1990
– Emily Thompson, *The Soundscape of Modernity: Architectural Acoustics and the Culture of Listening in America*, Cambridge, MA: MIT Press, 2002

When I first entered this church I saw the rhythm of the internal architecture shorn of all superfluity, with none of the gilt and ornamental trimmings of the Baroque style. I saw the severity of line and the rhythm of this vaulted construction, which reminds me so powerfully of the rhythm of Bach's music. It seemed to me that I had found the right place. MSTISLAV ROSTROPOVICH

BUILDINGS AND PROJECTS

SOUNDSPACE ARCHITECTURE FOR SOUND AND VISION

HELSINKI MUSIC CENTER
Competition, Finland, 1999

The entry is for the first stage of a two-stage competition to design a new music center in central Helsinki. The first stage focuses on the urban fabric and the planning of the site, the second on the architectural design of the buildings.

Although this stage of the competition is chiefly concerned with urban design, the proposed solution searches for ways to relate the building to its contents. Ultimately, it is more interested in developing a methodology connecting the general analogy between music and architecture with the site-specific circumstances of this particular project.

The program includes a symphonic concert hall, several smaller halls for performances and rehearsals, a music school, and public spaces such as an information center and a large lobby. The Helsinki Philharmonic, the Radio Orchestra and the Sibelius Academy will be the main users of the facility.

The music hall will accommodate concerts currently held at the neighboring, highly acclaimed Finlandia Hall, designed by Alvar Aalto. On the other side of the site is architect Steven Holl's Kiasma Art Museum, the central train station to the east and the Finnish parliament building to the west.

A master plan for the site and the surrounding areas had been designed, though never built, by Alvar Aalto. It is a currently underused key location in the city of Helsinki, and it connects the urban center with the park-like cultural row, and the lake beyond.

SÉRACS

CONCEPT

Two starting points were used to generate site and building design simultaneously: a subjective analysis of classical
and modern Finnish music by means of computation; and
research into the movements and behavior of glaciers.

In an effort to extract the substance of the two themes,
which are central to the project and the landscape of the
site, the two sets of findings were then merged. The result
has shown the possibility of creating a cohesive structure
across these two different investigative planes.

Common elements found in the underlying structures were
used to create form.

The merging of these elements with the real urban
conditions of the site and the programmatic analysis
shaped the project.

MUSIC

Rigorous analysis and interpretation of the internal structure of both classical and modern Finnish music were carried
out with a view to extracting the essence of this unique
cultural context.

A number of operations were performed on a variety of levels
in order to accommodate programmatic requirements both
on-site and off while bringing out the site's specific potential.
The program will not remain static or fixed in a traditional
sense but will depend dynamically on urban influences.

A type of "open city programming" has thus been applied
that supports the complexities of a rapidly evolving modern
city such as Helsinki, while also addressing the classical
roots of its past.

GLACIERS

Finland's geography has been formed by glaciers.

The arrangement and interrelationship between the building
blocks and their relationship to the site and the surroundings is informed by an analysis and interpretation of glacial
structure, form and movement.

Guiding principles and strategies:
> ice never sleeps;
> glaciers are rivers of ice,
> perfectly plastic yet solid – capable of cracking,
> deformation, and flow.

Form creation:
> glacial polish, striations; glacial erosion
> cirques: glacially eroded basins
> arêtes: jagged, narrow ridges
>
> glacial drift, debris
> lateral and terminal moraines formed
> by glacial movements
> erratic boulders: moved by glaciers
>
> séracs: pinnacles of ice formed where the
> glacier surface is rent by serial crevasses

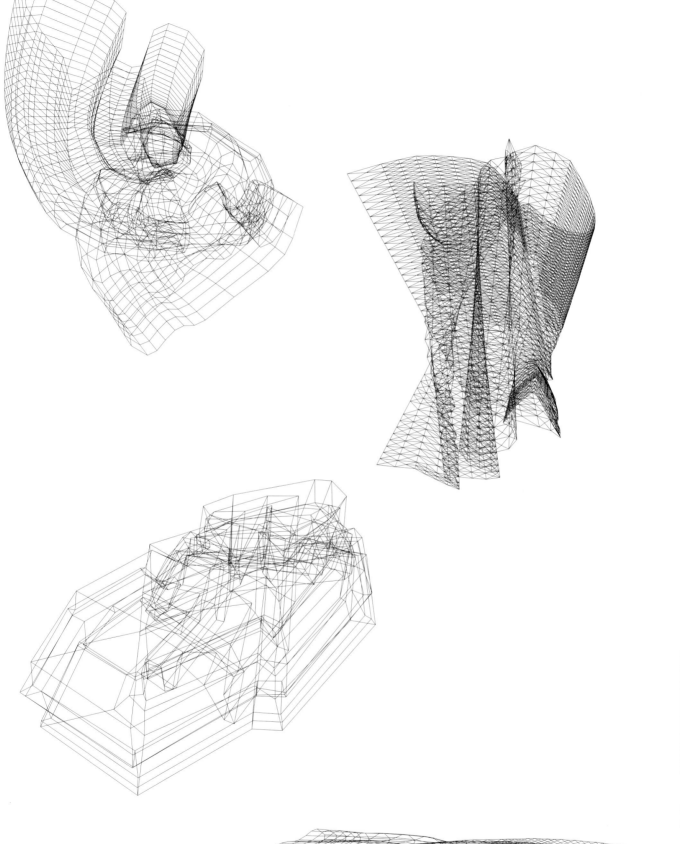

SOUNDSPACE ARCHITECTURE FOR SOUND AND VISION

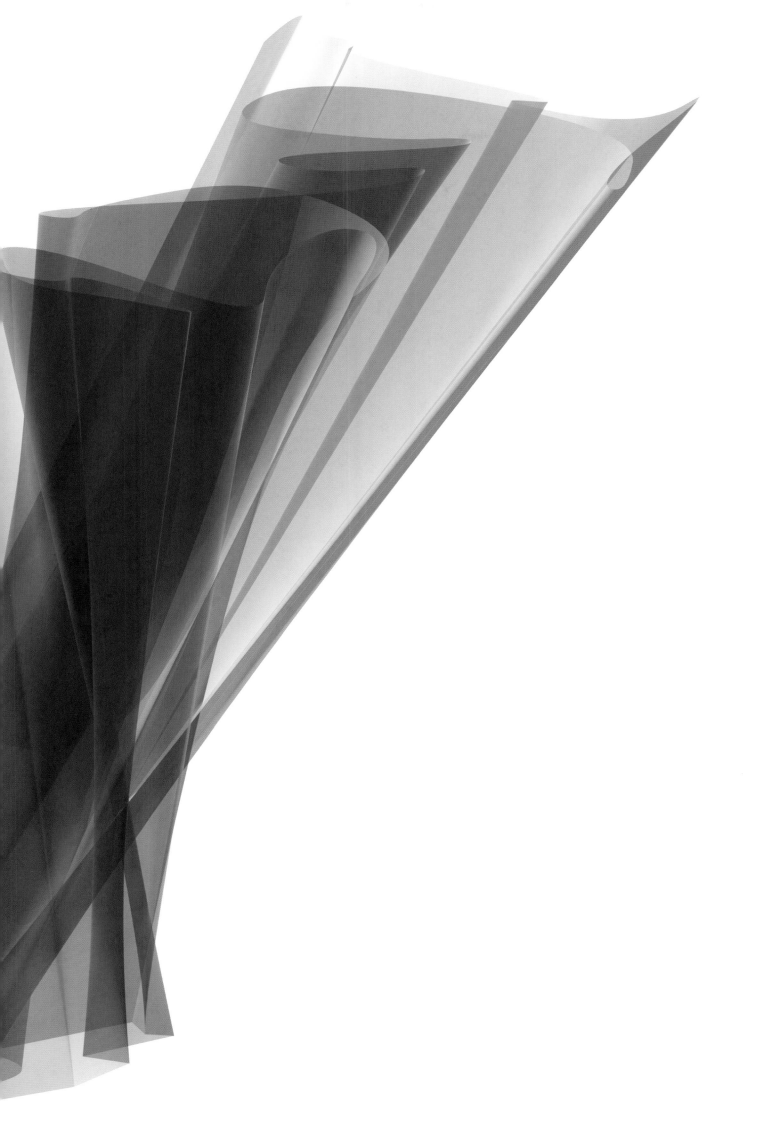

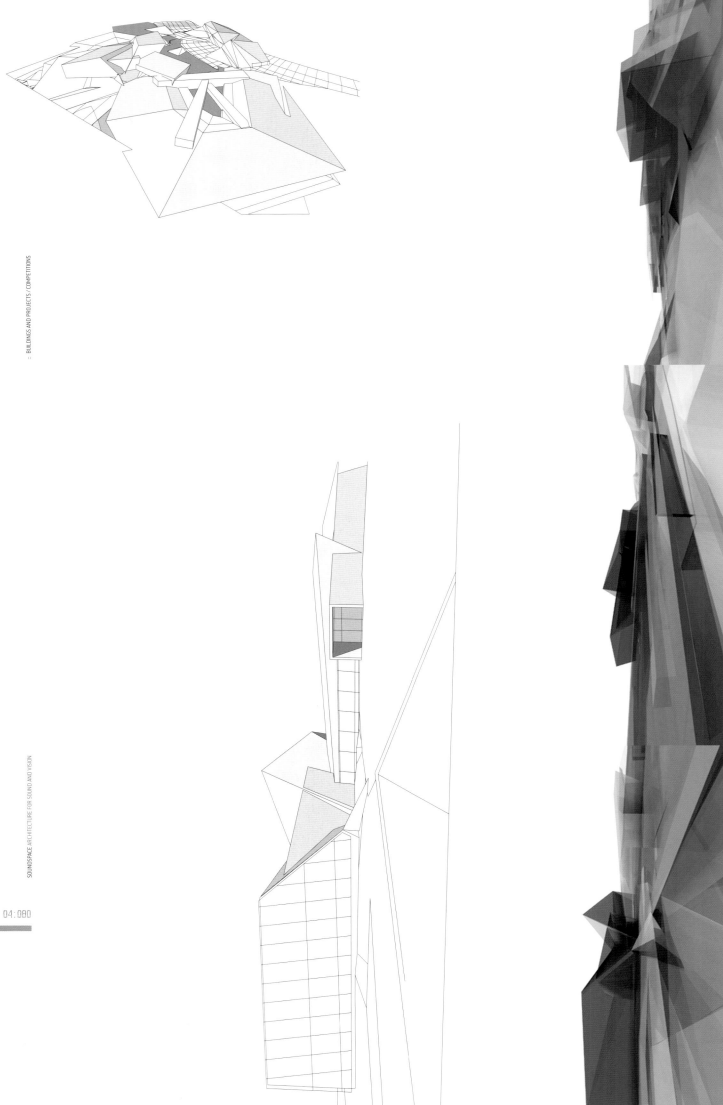

SOUNDSPACE ARCHITECTURE FOR SOUND AND VISION

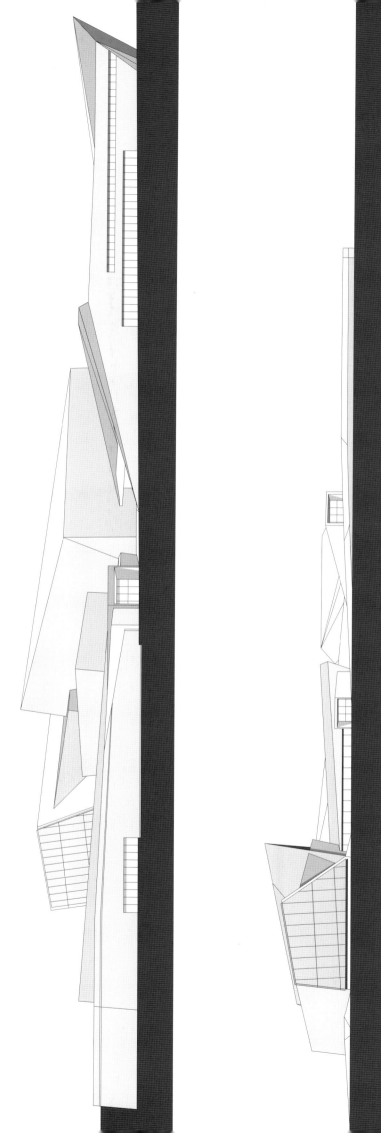

SOUNDSPACE ARCHITECTURE FOR SOUND AND VISION

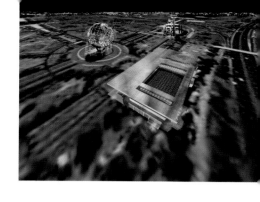

QUEENS MUSEUM OF ART

Competition, New York, 2001

The role of contemporary art juxtaposed with the history of the site creates an energized combination. The notion of disparate groups coming together through curiosity is common to both the World's Fair and contemporary art. Architecture performs an analogous critical examination of the existing conditions on the site by exploring varied thinking and goals. These influences evoke a design for the QMA which mediates between the past and the present while looking vigorously to the future.

Through a reductive process, the existing shell founds a new design strategy. It has been eroded to perform as a permeable enclosure that is able to support a flexible framework for exploration and experimentation.

The floating roof plane performs as an overturned plaza, publicly accessible and expansive. Spatially inclusive, it draws the exterior into the museum and the interior outward. It anchors the building visually while including the surrounding site, thus creating a variety of public spaces.

The inserted volumes are localized nodes of potent activity set into the framework of the existing shell. They structure both horizontal and vertical traffic through the exhibit galleries. Their simple forms complement the complex content of the museum exhibits.

Together, these elements combine into a design that promotes the contemporary agenda of art through versatility of space and thought. The creation of flexible spaces addresses the need for this type of venue and facilitates cross-pollination between varied experiences.

Selective design strategies achieve the spatial transformation into a dynamic environment for contemporary art, media and performance. The expansive floating roof, the exposed building skeleton, the red boxes, the terraces, the opened-up interior – all subvert existing conditions to create a new physical reality throughout and beyond the building. The result is a variety of anchored and defined spaces that allow constant change and surprising juxtapositions.

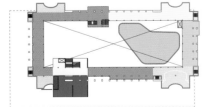

The front plaza is spatially appropriated to the museum without physical intervention on the ground level. The roof plane offers itself for integration into site-specific art or as a surface for media presentations.

Over too many cups of Sake, much displeasure was expressed at the contrived sound of too many modern recordings, not to mention the sterile atmosphere of too many modern recording studios. [...] After seeing dozens of Dance Halls, Theatres and so on, the final choice was an ancient Masonic Lodge, normally used by neighbouring Vanguard Studios for classical recordings. The explosive sound of this stone-and-wood hall can be heard on tracks such as *The Verdict* and *Be My Number Two*, simply picked up by a pair of vintage Neumann M-50 Microphones 15 feet in the air. [...] But every step of the recording process is no more than a step towards the ideal presentation of what really matters: the songs.   JOE JACKSON

MUSIC STUDIOS

Music recording studios occupy a special position within the array of media production facilities. Their singleminded devotion to the goal of superior acoustic performance makes their function more specific than that of any other program. Focused as they are on this unique and singular purpose, they have even stricter and more elusive requirements than mixed-media facilities. While various multimedia formats are now the standard for most forms of entertainment, pure audio still stands out for its emotional and creative potential.

Sound is a component of most media production formats today, from movies and television to video and computer games. The variety of delivery formats has resulted in a range of quality levels required for sound. Pure music recording studios need to achieve the highest level of sonic performance.

It is the music studio that has achieved mythical stature among production facilities. The Beatles, walking across the street in front of the Abbey Road studios in London, made that facility known far beyond recording industry insiders. The Beatles' emphasis on the studio also signals the importance of that particular working environment for the making of their records in those days. And indeed new technologies, like multitrack recording, had an impact on the artistic expression of music during those years that went beyond anything heard before. In the United States, the old Record Plant in Los Angeles became synonymous with rock 'n' roll's perceived excesses in the 1970s, featuring hot tubs and never-ending parties, and making music recording part of a particular and somewhat mythical lifestyle.

Opinions about different studio design philosophies can reach fanatical levels, and the rise of "black magic" acousticians during the early decades of this building type around the mid-twentieth century is no coincidence. With a propensity to obscure the science and to distract from a repeatable formula, some rather dubious acoustic theories have been proposed since that time. Contributing to the variety of different concepts is the notoriously difficult prediction of acoustical performance. The small scale of most projects does not allow the amount of research invested in, for example, concert halls or theaters, and for an entirely scientific design methodology.

On the other hand, existing studio designs based solely on scientific findings and laboratory research have not generally been too successful either. Generalized acoustic theories are often impractical due to limited space, construction budgets, and simply the necessary human presence and the ergonomics of operating equipment and occupying the spaces.

Most successful studio projects are conceived more pragmatically, mixing an understanding of the music production process, empirical knowledge of the requirements, basic acoustic theory, a concern for ergonomics and a sense of the spatial and architectural environment.

Generally, music studios are divided into two specialized areas, each with very distinct purposes: the actual recording rooms, where sound is created and captured, and the control rooms where it is monitored and controlled, and can be manipulated or mixed later. While other configurations exist and function in some instances, that combination is the proven standard today.

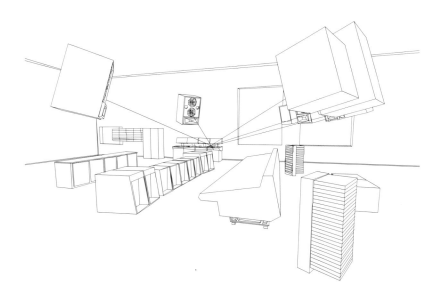

Recording spaces are related to familiar music spaces, such as concert halls, jazz clubs, rock arenas or other performance venues. Distinguishing them is the general lack of an audience and the different nature of the music-making itself. The temporal immediacy of a live performance is replaced by the relative permanence of committing the sound to a medium, and preserving it for future use.

To facilitate later manipulation, instruments and musicians are often in separate rooms, performing either simultaneously or at different times. This presents new challenges to artists interested in maintaining the freshness of a live recording.

As Emily Thompson has pointed out in her book,[1] developments in modern sound technology created a new acoustic paradigm in the twentieth century: clear and controlled, direct and non-reverberant sound denying the space in which it was produced. This shift in emphasis culminated in contemporary digital music production, where physical space is no longer even part of the process, and is replaced entirely by electronic samples and computer-based composition.

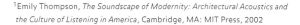

[1] Emily Thompson, *The Soundscape of Modernity: Architectural Acoustics and the Culture of Listening in America*, Cambridge, MA: MIT Press, 2002

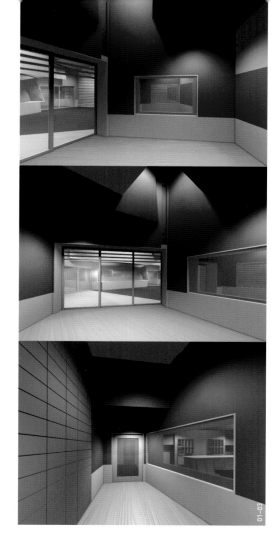

Contrary to these trends, the use of real physical space with audible acoustic properties is still regarded as an asset by many musicians and engineers. It is these artists who gravitate to studios with their preferred acoustic properties, and possibly variable acoustics. Or if they cannot find what they need, they move to other acoustic spaces to record their music. To them, their physical environment is still essential acoustically, architecturally and creatively, in order to achieve that indefinable "realness."

The second component of a traditional studio, the control or mix room, allows the discrete monitoring, and later the manipulation, of the recorded sound. Made essential by multitrack recording, these spaces are defined by the actual recording process and the applied technology. Their main purpose is really a physical impossibility: to play back sound exactly the way it is stored on the tape or the hard disc, without any interference from the room in which it is played.

Highly specific environments, these spaces are geared entirely to the reproduction of sound, eliminating as much as possible the effects of their boundaries, such as walls and ceilings.

Other spaces described in the following pages include music writing or composition rooms, and pre-production rooms, both used at the beginning of the process. Mastering rooms are dedicated to adding the final touches to the recording, and are conceptually more related to audiophile music listening rooms at the consumer level.

The projects in this book are designed within basic acoustic theory, with a good dose of empirical knowledge, a taste for improvisation and, most importantly, common sense. They do not fundamentally distinguish between acoustic and architectural design. Each project is approached as an architectural design problem, complemented by some basic theory of studio design and acoustics. The ultimate goal of this approach is to design spaces that are pleasing not just to the ear and the microphone, but to all human senses.

In the early years and decades of recording studio design there was a remarkable lack of interest in the visual or architectural aspects of these facilities. They were initially conceived as purely functional spaces. In the 1970s a typical, warmer studio style emerged and was widely accepted. Even today, possibly out of nostalgia, studios are being built that resemble relics from 1973. While that may have been the appropriate environment for a certain time and style, we believe that a contemporary but timeless environment serves the purpose better. The following projects aim to reflect the diversity and vitality of music in general. They are designed to provide a space that supports the creative process, that is modern and dynamic, and that can adapt to future developments.

Finally, it would be irresponsible not to point out the current predicament of music recording in general. While the recording studio business seems to be cyclical, a more serious downturn for commercial studios, already weakened by the continued trend of cheaper digital equipment and the growth of home studios, is currently taking place. The possibility of sharing electronic files for free is hurting the music industry, and by extension also the artists and studios. While file-protection systems are being developed, a real paradigm shift in the way music is paid for is happening. Along with smaller budgets, using real physical space for musical recordings is becoming a luxury many can no longer afford.

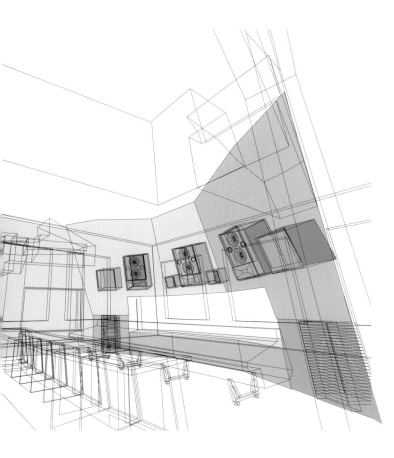

01–03 Sony Music Entertainment, Japan, Computer Renderings

BAD ANIMALS – STUDIO X
Seattle, Washington, 1992

Built by the Heart group in partnership with an existing production facility, the studio was always intended to be available, beyond its personal and commercial use, to the local symphony orchestra and to other cultural institutions. During the initial period of Seattle's growing grunge music scene, the city also needed a high-end studio facility to provide the necessary support for local recordings.

The project includes a music recording studio with a control room and a large "live" space, several isolation rooms for piano and vocals, two lounges – one for artists and one for staff – and support areas containing bathrooms, machine and computer rooms. The objective was to integrate the new studio into a former video shooting stage within the operating facility, but to allow its completely independent operation, as well as to set a new, contemporary standard for the interior and acoustical design of the facility.

The design needed to be functionally flexible. It was necessary for the spaces to be large enough to accommodate an entire orchestra, yet remain acoustically intimate, suitable for live recordings with just two or three musicians. The music would vary as well, from classical to jazz and rock 'n' roll.

Particular attention is paid to the acoustic performance of each room, with design elements serving sonic as well as aesthetic functions. The slat resonators in the studios and control room are tuned to the specific resonant frequency of these rooms. The wood panels shielding the studio curtains in their retracted position are angled to eliminate parallel wall surfaces, and are framed with a variably spaced support system to avoid duplicate panel resonances. The soffits surrounding the large tracking room space act as bass traps, eliminating excessive low frequency build-ups in the room corners. The undulating "ceiling cloud" in the studio was crafted from laminated plywood ribs and vacuum-formed maple panels by a local shipbuilder. Its sinuous rhythm brings to mind images of water and music. The fabric-covered frames, white-stained maple panels and slats, with their exposed steel frames and supporting elements, have a layered, repetitive quality that has definite musical connotations as well. The control room front wall, about twenty-two tons of concrete, is the first of its kind built in the United States. The raw concrete contrasts with the floating wood panels and fabric finishes on the other control-room walls.

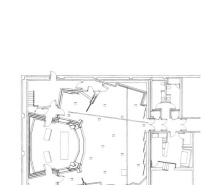

The exposed concrete front wall within the control room provides solid backing for the highly amplified speaker monitoring system, eliminating any resonances (left).

SOUNDSPACE ARCHITECTURE FOR SOUND AND VISION

Recording rooms of varying sizes, like the piano booth (top) and the main tracking space (bottom), are visually and spatially connected.

01-02

03–05

The undulating ceiling cloud (top) diffuses sound waves, with the focal points of the concave areas well above ear level. A low-tech curtain system permits musicians to vary the reverberation time within the studio space (bottom) to create the desired acoustical environment.

The most prominent element in the atrium space is the glass enclosure around the hot tub – a reminder of wilder days in the rock 'n' roll business. The glass enclosure can be screened off with blinds without shutting out the light from the skylights above.

01–04

THE RECORD PLANT
Hollywood, California, 1993

The Record Plant, founded in the late 1960s, and one of Los Angeles's most acclaimed recording studios, still enjoys a successful clientele of musicians, producers and sound engineers. Although the original facility was damaged in a fire and later closed down, a new location was opened a short distance away in 1986.

Before the featured expansion was built, the relocated facility contained two studios in a seventies-influenced, woodsy recording-studio style. After an ownership change in 1991, three more studios with support and leisure spaces were added within the existing building, a simple concrete-block and wood-truss structure.

The expansion introduced a different level of architectural expression to the facility and tied a fractured and incomplete plan into a whole complex of working and leisure spaces.

The centerpiece of the new portion of the facility, and the heart of the complex as a whole, is the large indoor atrium situated at the back of the building. The sixteen-foot-high ceiling in the atrium was rebuilt with two large skylights along the full length of the space, flooding it with daylight from the north. To emphasize the outdoor feeling, a number of elements surrounding the main volume are reminiscent of buildings around a town square. A client service counter, indicative of the attention paid to the customers, is clad in blue cement panels. A closed lounge is separated from the main space by a glass wall. A fountain and planter contribute to the casual sense of the space, and create a calming atmosphere for the kitchenette and bar.

The new studios are complete and self-contained work and relaxation suites, and include personal lounges and amenities.

The new main recording space is visually connected to the control room; both of these rooms are then similarly connected to a vocal booth for the recording of individual tracks. In the studio's raised ceiling, a beam remaining from the old structure is left exposed, and new acoustical block walls form the back corners and separated amplifier closets. The new mix room includes a vocal booth to the side, and a solid front wall, with a large, recessed TV screen. Like the control room, it can be used for post-production of film and TV soundtracks as well as straight music mixing.

With these improvements, the facility's reputation as the quintessential recording studio was restored, and the studio continues to attract "those who can go anywhere," as its slogan has it.

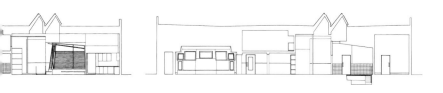

The introverted function of the mix room (top center) dictates the use of black fabric on the front wall. All attention in the control room (bottom) is focused on the tracking space beyond the glass, and on the loudspeakers arching over it.

05-07

The main tracking space is kept visually simple, to provide a neutral but comfortable working environment for the musicians, who often bring their own decorations. Deflection and resonator panels, slat diffusers/absorbers, and fabric-covered soffits control the acoustic environment.

01

02

X-ART STUDIOS
Pinkafeld, Austria, 1993

A rather unlikely location for a high-end recording studio, Pinkafeld is situated in the rural Burgenland province of Austria, about one hour by car south of Vienna. The two partners responsible both grew up in the area, and after successful careers as an electrical engineer and an audio-video specialist, returned to execute the project on their home turf.

Located halfway between Vienna and Graz, the studio is used by musicians from both cities. The facility serves the superb classical musicians of traditional Vienna, the thriving alternative songwriter and rock scene, as well as local Austrian folk-music groups. Post-production, multimedia and graphics services are also provided, and a portion of the building has recently been converted and is now used by a local radio station.

Set in a meadow amid grazing dairy cows, the building also houses a conference and training center, offering educational courses in the use of the various kinds of equipment.

Although a local architect planned the exterior structure, the studio shell was designed and built in a collaborative process to precise specifications, and freely made available to house the studio. The simultaneous design allowed for optimized dimensions and proportions of the layout.

This is a multi-use facility, so the acoustics were kept relatively reverberant, allowing for the easy addition of absorptive materials to alter the sound. Control of the sonic environment is achieved by means of a variety of wood and concrete reflection and diffusion devices, which also give the project its distinctive look and feel.

The name of the facility has recently been changed to The Mushroom.

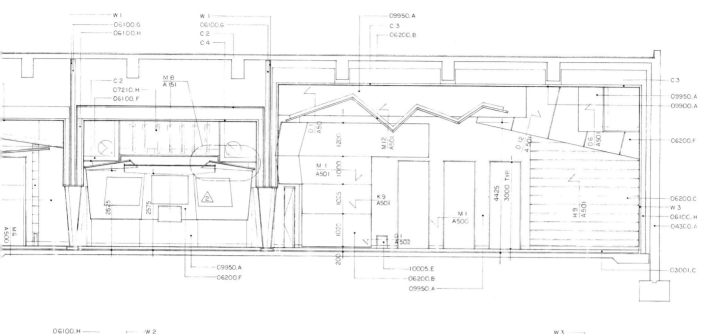

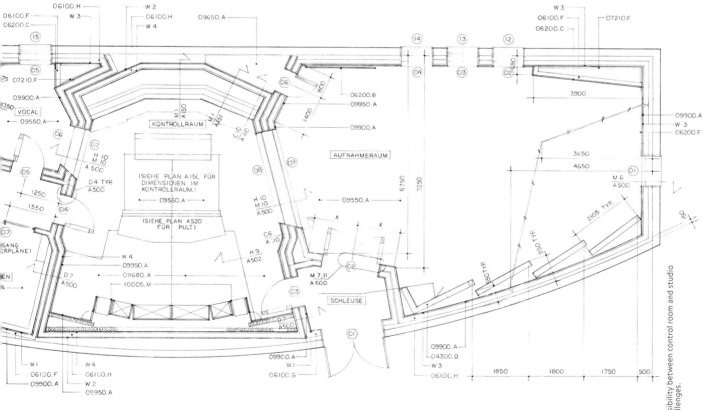

VOCAL

KONTROLLRAUM

AUFNAHMERAUM

(SIEHE PLAN A150 FÜR
DIMENSIONEN IM
KONTROLLRAUM.)

(SIEHE PLAN A520
FÜR PULT)

SCHLEUSE

Full-height glass maximizes the spatial connection and visibility between control room and studio space, but the large glass area poses some acoustical challenges.

04

The angular wood ceiling and wall panels dominate the reverberant acoustics and the visual characteristics of the tracking studio. Standard concrete block is used to form a slightly sound-diffusing pattern.

MEGA WEST STUDIOS
Paris, France, 1993

As one of Europe's main centers for music production, Paris has a thriving and very competitive studio scene. Mega Studios moved its operations from central Paris to the nearby suburb of Suresnes, close to the Bois de Boulogne, in order to enlarge and modernize its facilities. The new Mega West Studios now has several studio suites, the largest able to accommodate fifty musicians in its tracking space.

The industrial building provided the necessary heights, and the distinctive steel trusses allowed clear spans for the large rooms. The trusses were incorporated into the design and their filigree contributes to the light and airy atmosphere inside the studio. The spare and functional main space is lit with a continuous row of skylights, and the daylight is filtered into the adjacent control room and isolation booths.

Additional light enters through the second floor musicians' lounge overlooking the space. The connecting window juts out over the room, its frame and geometry reminiscent of the adjacent structural trusses.

The owner, a veteran speaker designer and acoustic perfectionist, designed the unusual array of subwoofers above the main loudspeakers in the control room. The twelve 16" low-frequency drivers of the subwoofers, together with the built-in surround-sound speakers and the requisite near-field monitors are amplified with a total of 9,000 watts of power.

The exposed concrete diffuser blocks help to control the acoustics in the relatively live tracking room. The lounge lets visitors overlook the space and delivers additional daylight to the room. The control room is set lower, with the eye level of the engineers slightly above the studio floor.

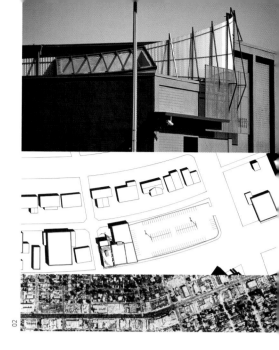

ROYALTONE STUDIOS
North Hollywood, California, 1995

As a new recording facility, conceived for the alternative rock bands of the owner's independent record label, the intention was to provide a hip atmosphere within an inspiring and comfortable working environment. Working with the acoustically specific architecture of recording studios, a great effort was made to utilize the necessary angles and materials to enhance the overall design intention of the project, while creating rooms that performed according to very particular acoustic needs.

The existing building's location at the only bend in the boulevard for miles in either direction inspired the use of an ellipse as a pivot point. Borrowed from the client's logo, an oblique view of a record album, the shape was then used as one of the main design elements in the project. It acts as a tie between interior and exterior, and integrates the new addition into the existing structure. Laid over the western portion of the building, it is a guideline for the design of various elements both inside and outside the building.

On the exterior the shape appears in the mechanical screen and skylight on the roof, in the curved cutout in the concrete-block wall of the tower, and in the back courtyard as a curved beam overhead and a pattern in the paving. Inside, the ellipse reappears in the spa skylight, the reception area stair and in the shaped ceiling and curtain rods of the main studio.

Given the sunny San Fernando Valley setting, the project allows as much natural light into the building as possible, with oversized skylights and glazed storefront systems opening to the exterior. With glass mostly oriented to the north, heat gain is nonetheless minimized. Light-pigmented plaster on the walls and ceilings reflects the light and changes color throughout the day.

While much attention was paid to the spatial development of the individual program parts, their interrelationships, and the natural lighting of the spaces, in the end it is the décor that is the most striking feature. All things gothic being a favorite theme of the late 1990s music scene, the atmosphere of a mock English castle has been transplanted into this Los Angeles facility, where it is combined with the technology and architecture of the late twentieth century.

The interior design, initially met with resistance from the architects, has ultimately been integrated, and the combination has proven a success with artists and engineers. In the end, the sumptuous luxury and the "vibe" of the place, with all its amenities and capabilities, constitute a truly memorable environment.

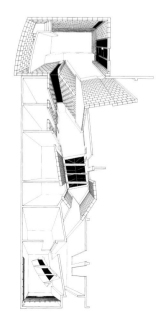

The spa, occasionally used as an auxiliary recording space, projects its angular cobalt blue walls up into the skylight, where they can be seen from the street.

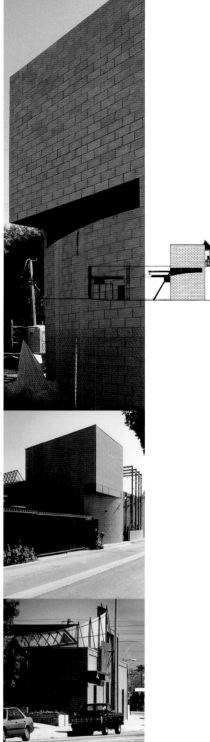

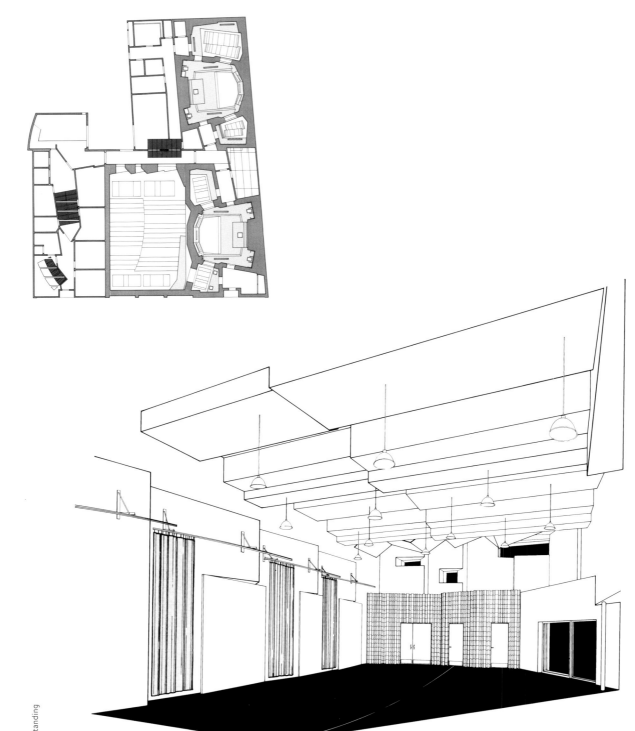

Here, during construction, the sculptural quality of the raw, still freestanding speaker wall can be better appreciated than in its final state.

Randomly placed openings (top) puncture the corridor and filter daylight into the inner spaces, including the traditionally dark studio areas. Various patterns of sound-diffusing and absorbing concrete block are used inside the studios, and repeated on the exterior. The owner's décor of medieval European themes is juxtaposed with a contemporary sensibility.

BRANDON'S WAY
Hollywood, California, 1996

A typical problem exists for recording studio projects in Los Angeles and else-where. The build-out and content of these buildings is by definition expensive and delicate, with high-profile owners and clients coming and going at all times of the day. On the other hand, real-estate and building requirements dictate locations in industrial and urban areas, where costs and available structures are more feasible.

This private production facility of one of the most accomplished composers, producers and artists in popular music fits that profile perfectly. The building faces a busy street and keeping a low profile with a simple, straightforward design is part of a strategy to avoid unwanted attention.

The respective requirements of occupants and technology led to a design with a cold, hard shell on the outside enveloping a warmer and softer inside build-out. The dichotomy between these two aspects is at the core of the design, as is the need to integrate highly technical equipment into a comfortable creative environment.

Responding to its context of stucco, chain link fences, utility poles and bill-boards, a perforated metal screen covers the front of the building, enclosing a planter and protecting new windows. Slightly angled, the screen sets up the acoustically derived angles within. Exterior walls are covered in smooth gray plaster, completing the monochrome scheme.

Inside, the dark gray floor plane continues, but is complemented by fabric panels, carpet, stained mahogany and bird's-eye maple, granite, aluminum and stainless-steel trim pieces. The proportions of the studio rooms are care-fully calculated, and acoustic devices are used throughout. Soffits give the rooms their shape and control the sonic performance. Low-frequency absorbers and acoustic diffusors are concealed there, as well as ductwork and lighting. A combination of hard and soft finish surfaces tune the rooms acoustically and give them their final appearance.

The entire facility is conceived to seamlessly integrate a highly complex and technical apparatus within a luxurious and enjoyable environment, yet remain hidden away from public view. The technological requirements of the equipment, the acoustics of the spaces, the ergonomics of the users, and the visual and spatial impact of the architecture are balanced to form a work-place conducive to the creative process of the artists.

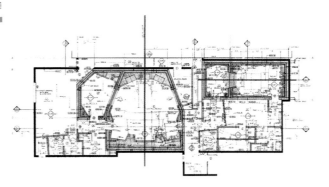

An existing brick corridor has been turned into a sunlit display of a large collection of awards.

Control room A is the heart of the facility (top, center), and serves a recording booth with a grand piano (far left). The B-suite (bottom) is smaller, but similar in appearance and performance.

Exterior detailing blends in with the light-industrial neighborhood.

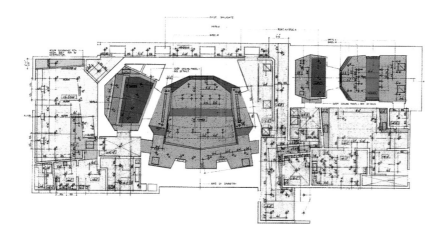

The rear lounge contains design elements derived from other parts of the building. The soffits of the acoustic rooms reappear here, to carve the room spatially and house ductwork. A large mechanical duct is left exposed in the space and a new sliding door, made of a galvanized steel frame with red-stained mahogany panels and typical off-the-shelf barn door hardware was added to an existing loading dock opening.

01

02

03–04

COUNTERPOINT STUDIOS
Salt Lake City, Utah, 1997

Salt Lake City in Utah, with its largely conservative population, is not known as a hotbed for cutting-edge music. Until this project was executed, the region had no world-class facilities for musicians to rehearse or record in. Nonetheless, there is a burgeoning scene of progressive musicians and bands in the city.

The two young partners in this start-up venture set themselves some ambitious goals, one of which was to provide a much-needed venue for the alternative music scene. The complete three-room commercial music recording facility is complemented by post-production, editing and graphics capabilities. Current projects include graphics for a feature-length animation movie, and a lot of audio post-production for film and television. Music recording and mixing remain primary activities in the studios, which now rival facilities in Los Angeles, New York or Nashville.

Engineers from the studio are engaged for location recording at an annual Salt Lake City classical piano competition. Recordings of all the participants' programs were made on the nine-foot Fazioli concert grand piano in the main studio, so demonstrating the versatility of the space.

An existing 5,000-square-foot light-industrial building, previously a printshop, was chosen as the site. The roof is a steel bow-truss structure, with a clear span across the width of the building. To claim all available height in the space, and to take advantage of the most interesting feature in the structure, the bow trusses were incorporated and left exposed.

Less than an hour away from some of the world's best powder skiing, and setting an unmatched standard for recording in the Wasatch Mountains region, the studio has all the makings of a winter resort facility.

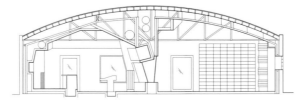

The main tracking suite consists of a 750-square-foot recording room, a large drum booth, and a separate vocal booth, all arranged around the generously sized control room. The spaces are connected and highlighted by the building's original steel trusses and concrete sound-diffusor blocks.

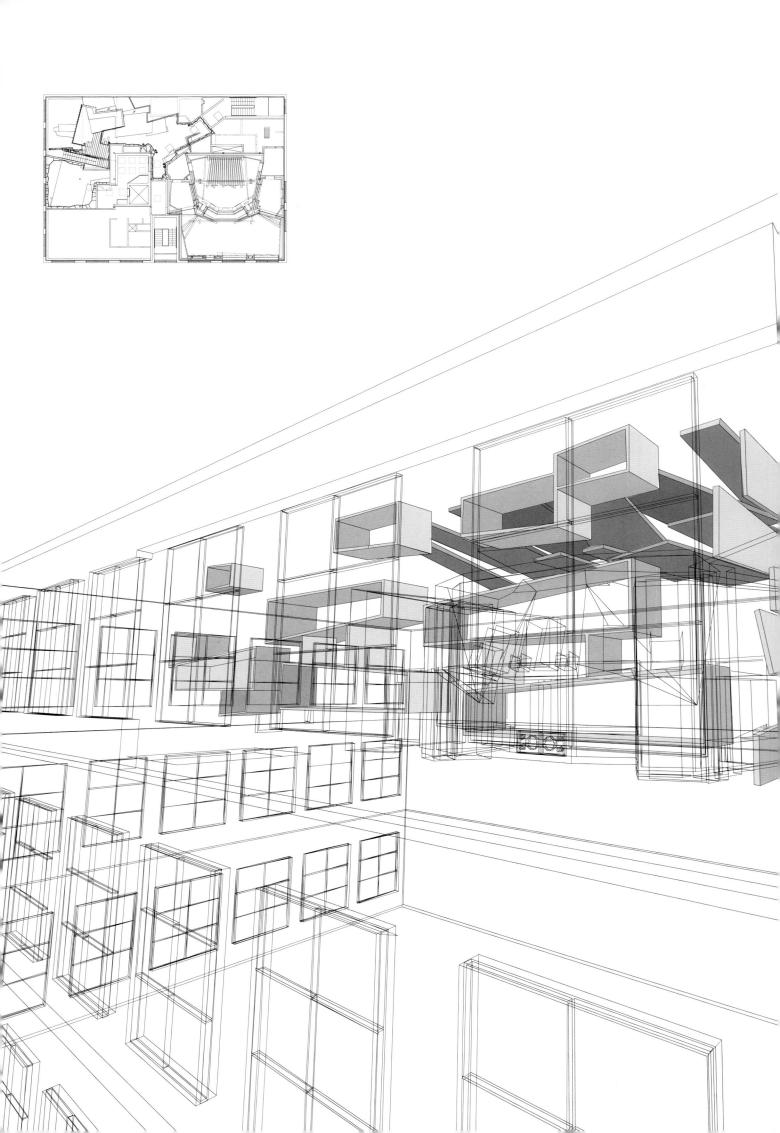

ROCKLAND STUDIOS
Chicago, Illinois, 1998

The attempt to reconcile contradictory program elements and client mandates into a cohesive contemporary solution dictates the main design concept for this project. The desired environment, described as a rustic landscape with an emphasis on rocks, trees and log-cabin structures, houses a fully functional music studio. The thematic environment cannot be allowed to compromise the demands of the recording equipment and its seamless integration into the building. As a result, the client's requests are elaborated upon, and compatible aspects of the theme are utilized to acoustical advantage. In the process, the superficial theme park approach is transformed into a comprehensive architectural concept, unifying form and function. The desired appearance is used as a fundamental structural element rather than applied as décor over an unrelated functional core.

Strict acoustic parameters and equipment requirements are paramount in the studio segment of the plan. In the control room, traditional log-cabin construction provides midrange sound diffusion on the back wall and ceiling, and structural support for the independently floating inner shell. The acoustic frequency response and the reflection patterns originating from the loudspeakers are directly related to the construction methods and materials.

The tracking room and the additional recording booths require high sound-isolation levels, and a strictly controlled acoustic environment. Rock walls, logs, floating wood panels and fabric-covered soffits are used to achieve this. Openings allow daylight into the studios, and form a new geometric layer superimposed on the inside of the large existing windows.

In the common areas, a cave of faux-rock walls is complemented by a more architectural arrangement of hard-edged tectonic concrete pieces. All rock elements and masonry walls are bordered by clean steel plates, exposing the stone's constructed quality. Logs recur here, and the materials and detailing further the precedent introduced in the acoustic spaces. Recessed video monitors and loudspeakers in the rock walls close the conceptual circle by recalling the environment's purpose as a high-tech production facility.

All of the existing large exterior windows are maintained, but wall layers with different window shapes are installed on the inside, making the transformation visible from the street, and filtering daylight into the spaces while enhancing the soundproofing of the studio.

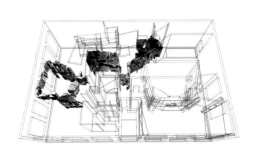

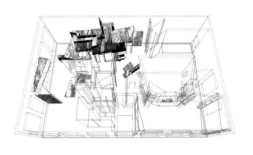

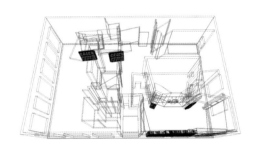

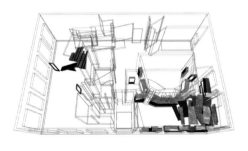

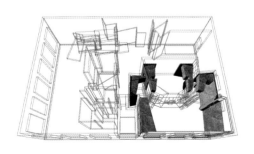

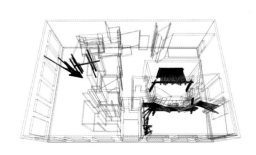

Material choices mandated by the thematic program are utilized to fulfill structural and acoustic demands throughout the facility.

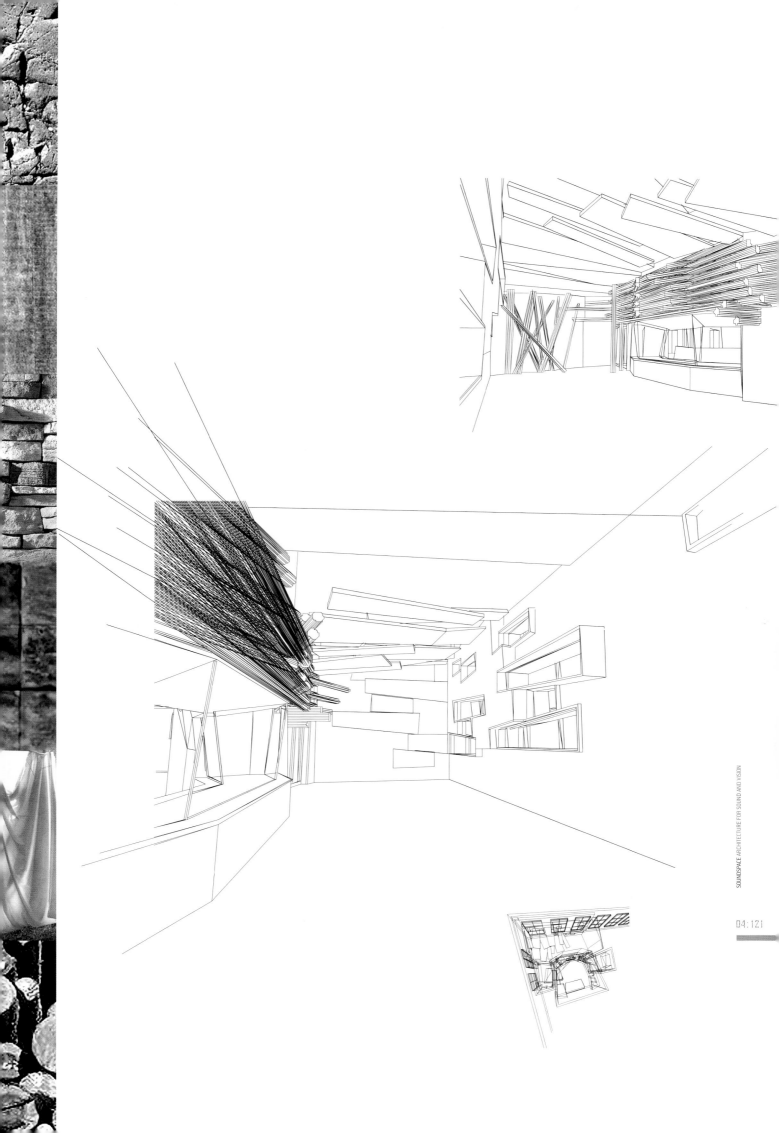

SOUNDSPACE ARCHITECTURE FOR SOUND AND VISION

04.121

SOUNDSPACE ARCHITECTURE FOR SOUND AND VISION

The loft overlooking the lounges is made of tectonic plates and rough wood boards, and is suspended from the roof structure for better load distribution. Built-in furniture throughout the public areas is made of smooth formed concrete.

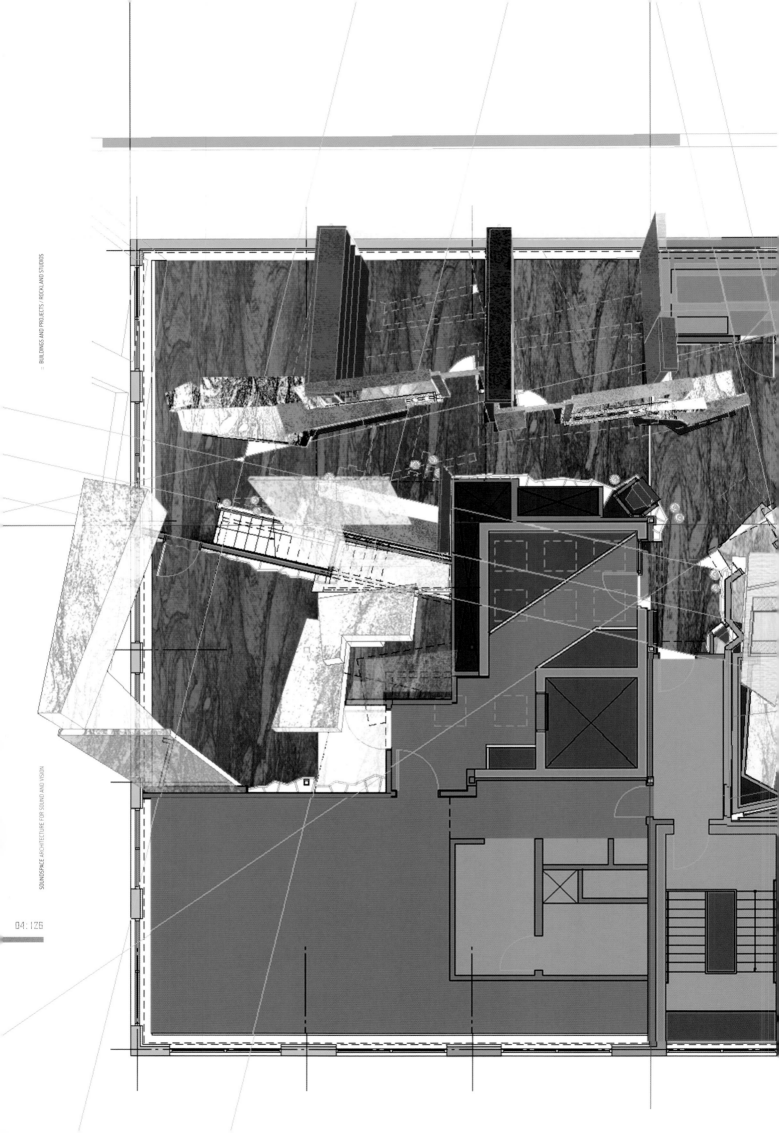

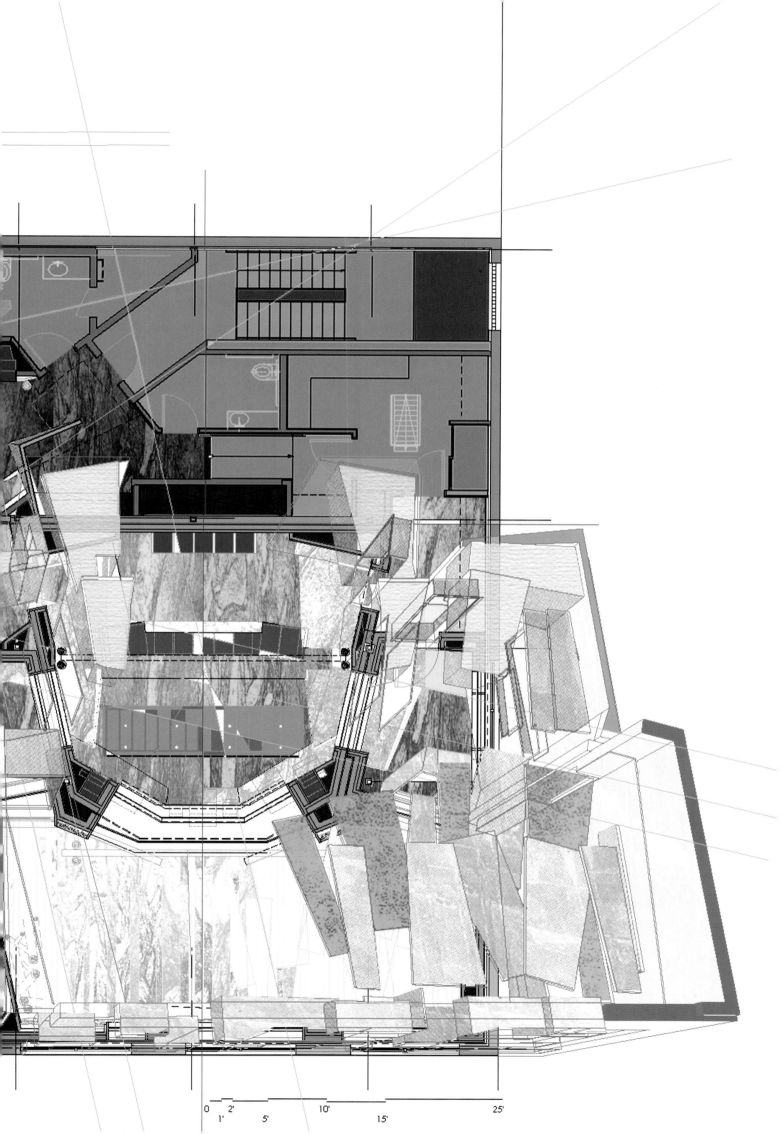

0 2'   10'   25'
   1'   5'   15'

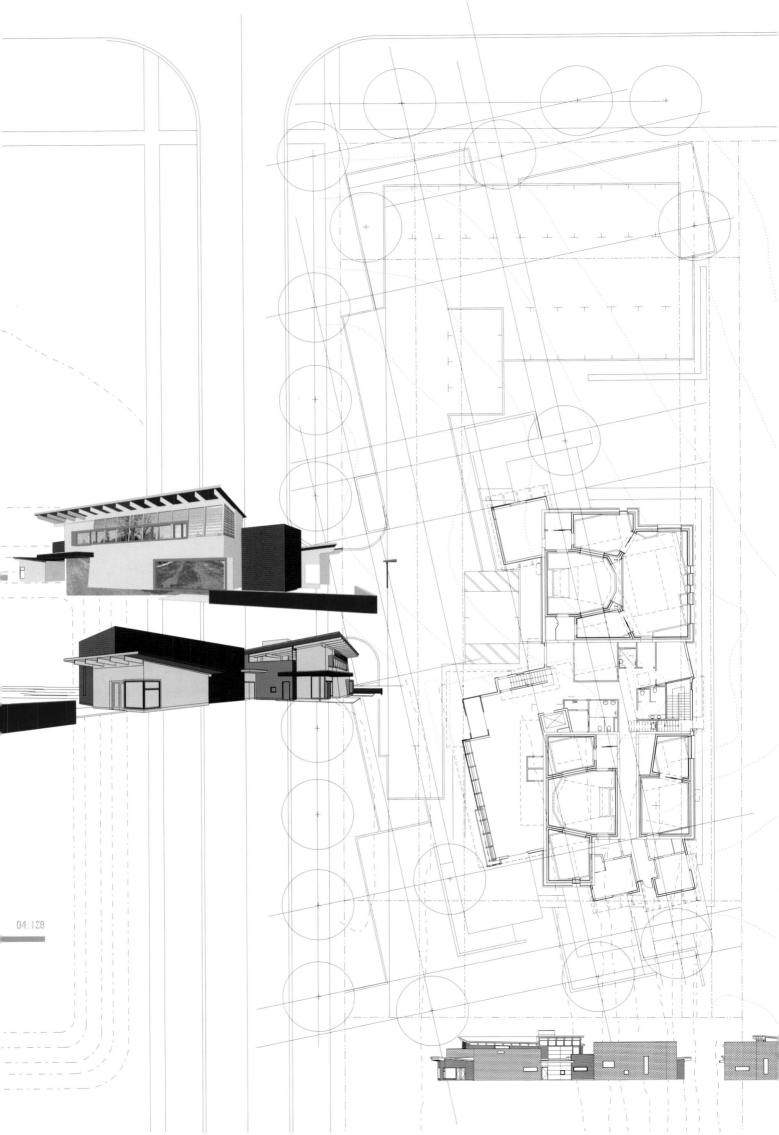

OUR HOUSE STUDIOS

Lemont, Illinois, 1998

The complex is located at the entrance to a new residential subdivision in the far southern suburbs of Chicago, and is part of a developing commercial strip along the main highway. The design guidelines and zoning laws governing the area require wide setbacks, utility easements, parking, and flood-control measures.

The design attempts to incorporate the open space around the building, and to connect the landscape to the interior as much as possible. The building is anchored into the expanse of the surrounding land by means of two overlaid grids, which extend over the entire property.

As the figurehead for the residential development, and its visual anchor in the area, the building asserts its presence with dynamic massing, bold colors and exposed constructive detail elements. The peripheral volumes all open up to the surroundings, and their roofs rise away from the core. The basic volumes are two L-shaped black concrete-block buildings, placed orthogonally to the street grid, and pierced only by small window openings. They house the main functions of the complex: three music recording studio suites with their auxiliary spaces. The concrete-block walls, though constituting the central mass for the composition of the volumes, also help provide the sound transmission values needed for the studios.

Between, around and inside the block buildings, the infill structure is differentiated by an alternate ordering grid, by the use of softer materials, and by a more open and transparent approach. The secondary grid also extends inside the block buildings to form acoustic soffits in the studios, and out into the landscape to further anchor the building to the land.

Lounges, restrooms, offices and a conference room are arranged on the first and second floors and made of wood framing, glass-and-cement panels and wood siding. Large windows open up to the landscape and are protected from the sun by wide overhangs and brise-soleils.

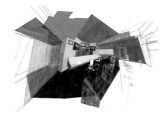

SONY MUSIC STUDIOS
Tokyo, Japan, 2001

The design and construction of a complete new live-music recording facility is a rare opportunity in the age of computerized digital sound production. The inclusion by Sony Music Entertainment Japan of this large project within their new headquarters demonstrates their commitment to live-music recording. As a result, the project revolves around studio spaces where musicians, instruments and sound engineers can still interact with their spatial environment.

Following an initial design competition, studio bau:ton teamed up with the Tokyo-based Obayashi Corporation. With Obayashi planning and constructing the building, bau:ton designed the 70,000 square feet of studio areas and key identifying features throughout the project. The ten-story building in the heart of Tokyo contains studio facilities on three basement floors and offices above the street level. Two large recording studios with control rooms and isolation booths, complemented by three mixing suites, provide a full-service recording complex on the bottom floor. Above, a total of eleven mastering and editing rooms are available for further processing of the recordings. The third studio level is occupied by New Media production, including spaces for video production and CD-ROM and DVD authoring. A "Liveteria" and a restaurant on the second floor provide space for band showcase concerts and hospitality events. These spaces were also designed by studio bau:ton, as was the signature security booth at the studio parking entrance. As the studio design architect, the team was involved in a truly interdisciplinary and international collaboration, bridging architecture, interior design, acoustics, furniture design, loudspeaker and product development.

These world-class studios represent the last word in state-of-the-art recording facilities. Spaces capture the sound produced by classical and contemporary instruments and musicians, while allowing current high-end technology to be used to its fullest potential from recording to mixing and mastering. While maintaining a separate identity from the corporate offices in the building, the studio areas are unified as an environment that enhances and supports the various phases of artistic creation and production.

The large studio tracking spaces are divided up by isolation booths and allow multiple recording configurations and sonic environments. Ergonomically designed control rooms provide accurate monitoring conditions and comfortable accommodation, and take into account possible future developments in equipment. The technical equipment and acoustic elements are incorporated into forms that express the complexity of the program, but mediate it with clean and simple detailing. Finishes in the studio areas emphasize natural materials. Granite floors and raw concrete block, beech-wood and fabric panels alternate with sintered aluminum and glass, along with bright color highlights.

Studio loudspeakers were custom-designed for this project in collaboration with TEC:ton sound systems. Acoustic diffusor elments were also custom-designed, and manufactured in Switzerland by paraDOX Acoustics. Equipment furniture was designed and built in Los Angeles before being shipped to Japan and installed by local carpenters.

The entry to the parking garage as it was designed and built (above). The elliptical security booth is tilted down from the street to guide visitors into the building.

The initial concepts for the project (these pages) were first worked out as part of an architectural competition in collaboration with the Taisei construction corporation. This scheme for the building was ultimately not used.

02-03

The executive dining room and the "Liveteria" (left) continue the theme of the studio design.

The main music studio level (plan, below) contains five recording and mixing suites (right and opposite page, top).

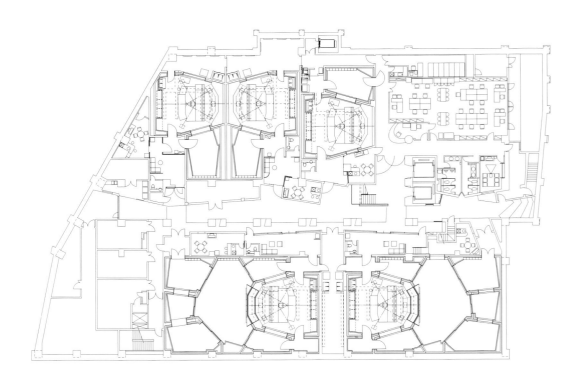

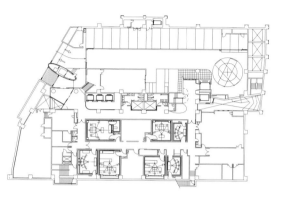

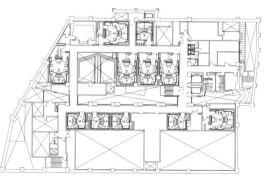

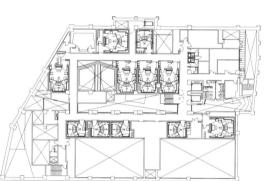

Mastering rooms, editing suites and new media production spaces on the upper two studio floors (plans above).

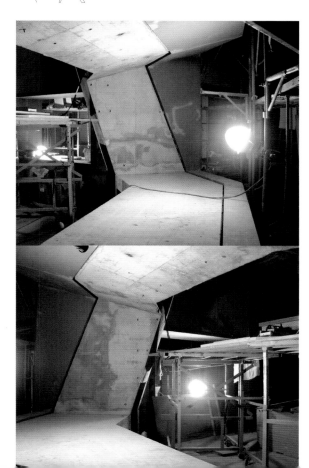

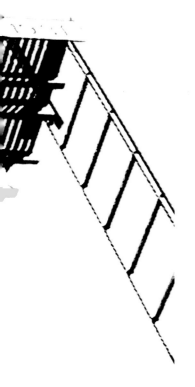

STUDIO ATLANTIS
Hollywood, California, 2000

The project site is a commercial storefront building with six original narrow bays in a rather unglamorous area of Hollywood. The starting point was an existing small recording studio in one of the bays; the project is the first phase of its upgrade and expansion into a world-class professional music recording and mixing suite. Future expansions are planned for the remaining bays of the building and in adjacent structures.

Surrounded by discount shoe stores, a pet store and adult entertainment establishments, the project adds a new, sophisticated element to the neighborhood. The necessity for tightly soundproofed spaces is contradicted by a relatively open front façade adjacent to a noisy thoroughfare. Another inherent contradiction exists between security concerns in a rough neighborhood and the desired visual connection to the outside. An industrial galvanized steel screen protects the storefront on busy Western Avenue, but behind it the main exterior elevation of the building offers the typical glazed façade to the street. The steel screen provides security and shade for the west-facing façade.

The search for an appropriate expression of the program and solutions to the technical problems were the main generators of the design. In addition to the client's requested water theme, the designers explored ways to express the ephemeral nature of sound, and methods to visualize the sonic forces shaped inside the studio spaces.

The studios are contained in a single volume inserted into the space. Within the exposed rough finishes of the old building, the luminous volume of the sound areas designates the special status and purpose of the high-tech sound processing facility.

Undulating translucent Lumasite panels wrap the studio exterior; the pattern is repeated inside for acoustical purposes. Expressing the power of the sound waves created within, the shifting and omnipresent studio box reacts to and informs the surrounding service areas.

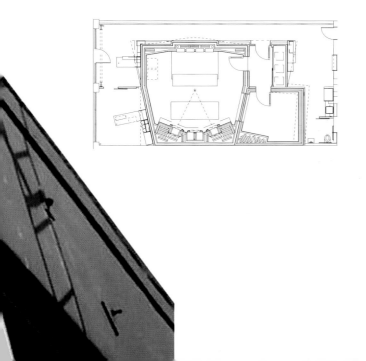

Circulation and common areas around the actual studio spaces are governed by the undulating skin wrapped around the contained volumes.

01–02

Materials and patterns are repeated throughout the facility. Daylight is brought in through skylights at strategic locations.

Strategically placed shelves and cupboards take advantage of the depth, where the undulating layers are pushed away from the hard shells behind.

New skylights have been cut into the roof to provide natural daylight and emphasize the volume of the studio suites. A dichotomy between dark, isolated studio rooms and light-flooded common areas creates a tension that reflects the working methods of artists and recording engineers.

The highly technical and accurate recording space and control room, along with the machine room at the core, are crucial elements of the design. Strict acoustic parameters and equipment requirements are paramount in the studio. The control room houses the central monitoring and mixing equipment, and its acoustic-frequency response and reflection patterns are carefully engineered. The tracking room requires even higher isolation levels, and a severely controlled acoustic environment.

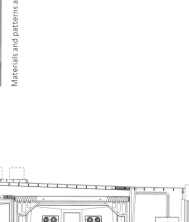

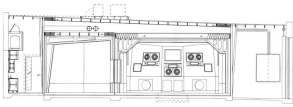

The studio becomes at once a musical instrument (reinforcing and aiding the sound generated by the musicians) and a machine for translating the sound into analog and digital information.

The technological complexity and necessary accuracy of the recording equipment and its seamless integration into the building are expressed here by the architecture of the studio environment.

SOUNDSPACE ARCHITECTURE FOR SOUND AND VISION

01

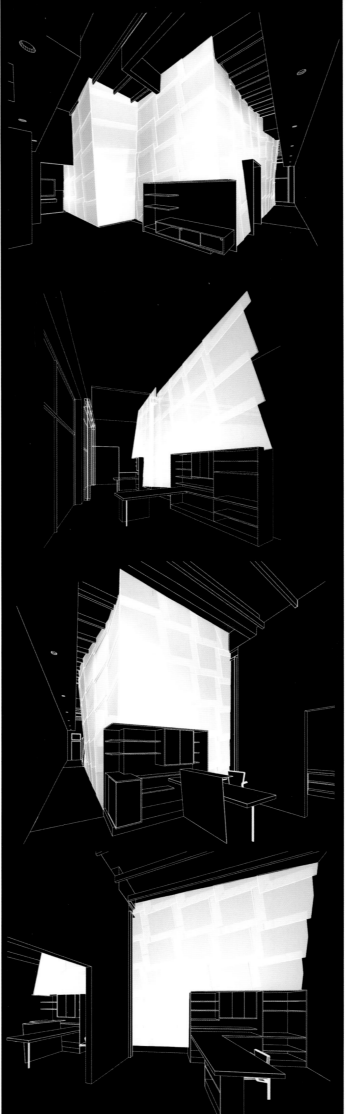

The translucent skin is punctured by built-in cabinetry, recapturing utilitarian space within a poetic concept.

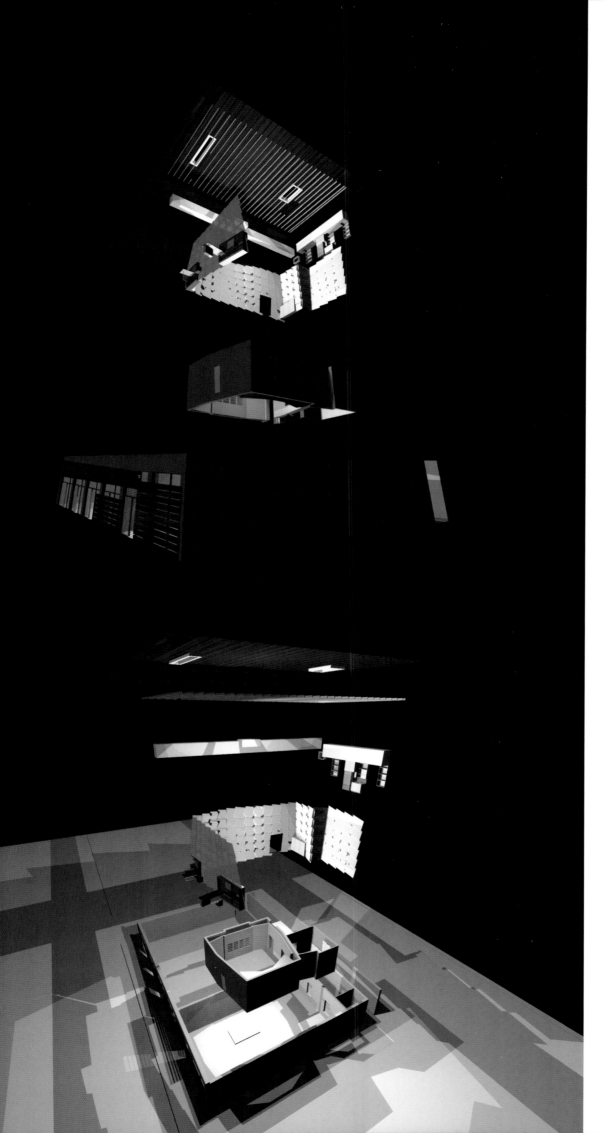

03

Phase two of the project, a lounge adjacent to the completed space, was finished in early 2003. Shapes and materials used in the first phase have been continued and will connect the studio to phase three, already planned for the building's remaining spaces. The large, warped plane of the wall finish turns into a ceiling.

The warped planes and shingle patterns of the outer skin are also used for acoustical purposes within the studio area. A complete surround-sound system is built into the room.

01–03

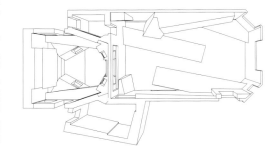

STUDIO 1314 MELISMA RECORDS
Atlanta, Georgia, 2000

This unbuilt project for a recording studio complex is located in a suburban industrial area west of downtown Atlanta; mixed uses in the area include manufacturing, distribution, printing plants, railroad yards and water treatment plants. The character of the surroundings, with its low density and random assemblage of utilitarian buildings in the landscape, inspired the massing and materialization of the project.

The site includes an existing two-story office building, with an earlier addition of a large hall used as a private recording and rehearsal space by a local gospel group. Adding the new building area triples the project's size. The client, a composer and producer in the alternative rock music scene, planned to occupy the building for the creative, production and managerial aspects of his company's work. Use by outside clients was also envisioned.

The particular need for a stimulating creative environment demanded transformation from a derelict shell into a sophisticated building using the simplest means available. As much of the project was to be new construction, the conceptual layout directly addressed the functions of each architectural element. Pinwheels and stacks of simple blocks were inspirations for the massing. Isolated sound areas are spatially separated and contained within their own concrete-block boxes, with few natural connections to the outside. Sound isolation had to be achieved without excessive construction, and the plan simplifies the detailing. Strong emphasis is placed on the live room acoustics of the recording spaces, the integration of the technological requirements, and the creative environment for the artists and engineers. The purpose of the studio as a state-of-the-art recording complex is paramount, but just as much attention is directed to the natural lighting and spatial compositions.

Recreational spaces with various degrees of privacy are needed throughout the building and outdoors. Common spaces are free-flowing and open, emphasizing the relationship to the outside landscape. Here the placement of large openings and natural lighting is a priority.

Conceptual sketches and natural lighting studies for the main tracking room (left). Acoustical study models (right).

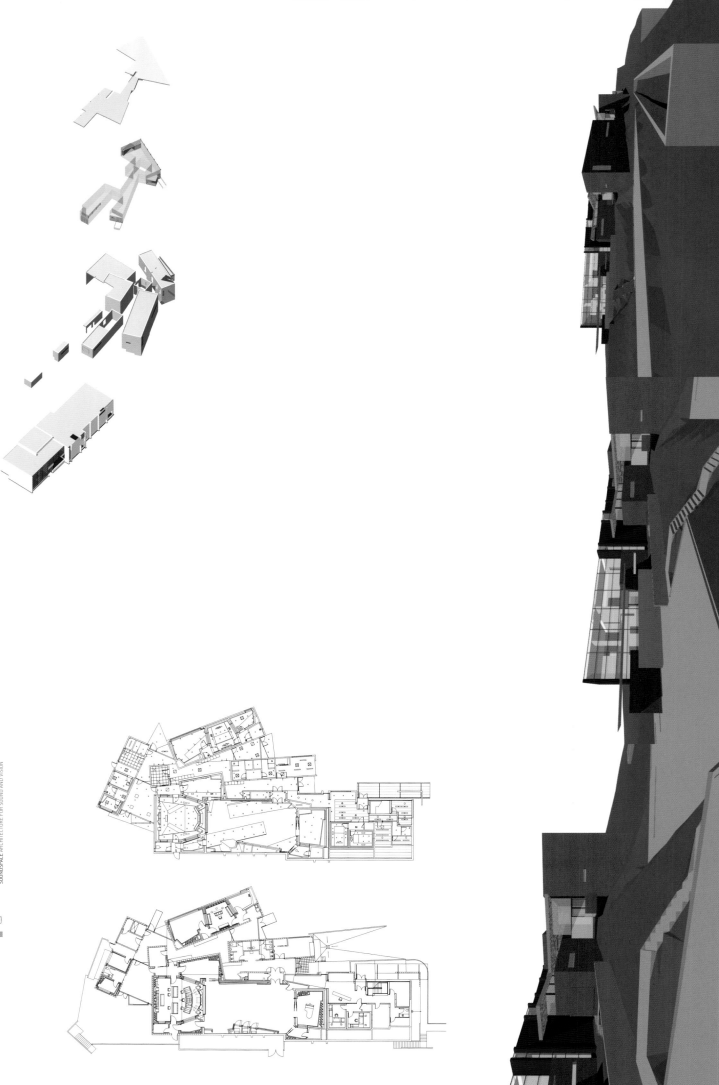

SOUNDSPACE ARCHITECTURE FOR SOUND AND VISION

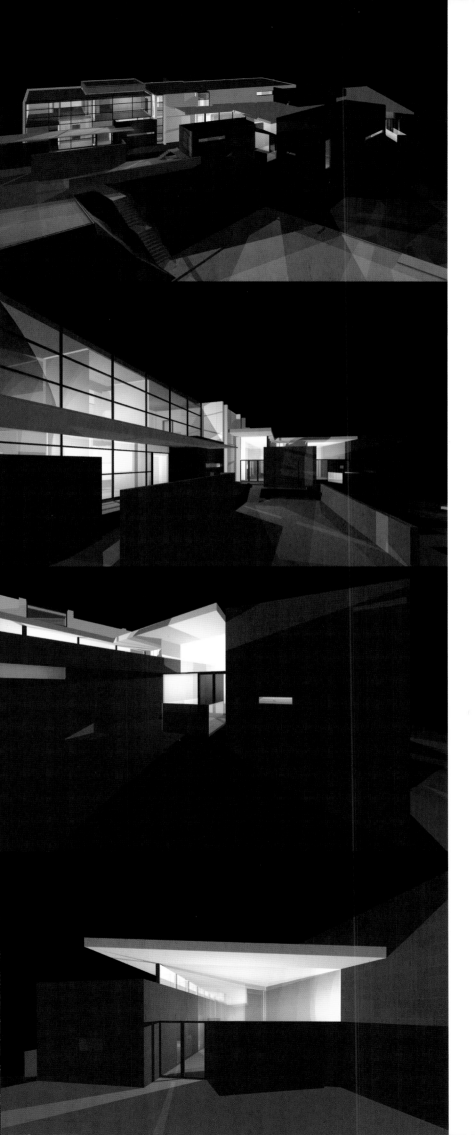

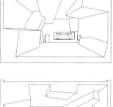
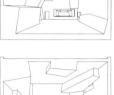

LUMINOUS SOUND
Dallas, Texas, 1999

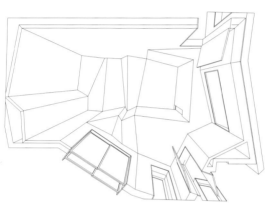

The relocated studio facility for Loomis Productions supports an advertising agency and a music and film production company. The practical requirements were simple: the creation of no-frills production studios to record and produce commercial jingles. But the owner's personal interests and credentials (as a multi-platinum producer, jazz songwriter, film director and composer) called for at least one serious live-music studio.

The 6,500-square-foot ground floor space now hosts three recording studios, complemented by office space on the upper level. The architectural layout for the facility evolved during a lengthy collaborative process, which included evaluating perhaps a dozen floor plans. In the final scheme, the complete audio suites fit within the confines of the space with nearly optimum room sizes, shapes and adjacencies.

The heart of the project, and its showpiece, is the main tracking room, which extends up into the second floor and thus occupies a double-height space. A window on the office floor allows a glimpse of the studio work from above, and integrates the facility's activities.

The room's exciting angular geometry is emphasized with finishes of clear maple panels and bright red wall fabric. The sharply angled panels avoid parallel surfaces and deflect sound waves, while shaping the visual character of the space. Most importantly, the size and shape of the room, and its acoustical design, allow serious live tracking sessions, from rock bands to jazz and classical orchestras. Additional isolation booths adjacent to the main space permit separate recordings of piano, vocals or drums, increasing flexibility of use.

Although it was not the primary objective of the project, the new space has enjoyed a fully booked program of live recording sessions with well-known musicians and bands.

TK DISC STUDIOS
Honolulu, Hawaii, 1999

The concept of a resort studio, where musicians can work undisturbed, away from city stress, is an especially alluring one. To make a great record, and relax in a beautiful, exotic locale while doing so, is a tempting proposition. For all that, however, there are not too many examples of successful resort studios around the world. One reason is the shrinking of record production budgets; another is the difficulty of operating a highly technological facility far away from the necessary support and maintenance structure.

Hawaii, though not exactly an underdeveloped island, is nonetheless located in the middle of the Pacific Ocean, three thousand miles from Los Angeles. That may be the reason for the lack of any great commercial facility on the islands until recently.

TK Disc Studios is a complete music recording and production studio, conceived by Japanese producer, musician and composer, Tetsuya Komuro. Aware of the natural beauty of the island and its attraction to many artists, he chose to relocate his operations to Honolulu. The site is a former restaurant building in a shopping center outside Honolulu, adjacent to a private waterway. The existing building shell had to conform to the mall's standard and could not be changed substantially, but the new construction nonetheless required the rebuilding of large structural parts. Limited room for the program and the studio's sound isolation and acoustic performance requirements led to a split of the studio suites between the two floors for optimum horizontal and vertical adjacencies. The demand for enclosure in the studio spaces had to be reconciled with the advantages of the unique site by the water and the strong Hawaiian light.

The design attempts to reconcile the new intensive uses with the existing conditions, and to create coherence without extensive changes to the building.

The facility is now called Avex Honolulu Studios, after a recent ownership change.

A tilted glass cube marks the entrance, which was moved from the parking lot to the water's edge to create a better access point to the building and a more pleasant entrance sequence.

01

02–05

To create a sense of consistency, the individual soffit volumes maintain their materiality and color where they appear throughout the building. The volumes are used to control the sonic performance of each studio room. Large windows connect the reclusive studio environment with the Hawaiian landscape and tropical light outside.

06

07

SOUNDSPACE ARCHITECTURE FOR SOUND AND VISION

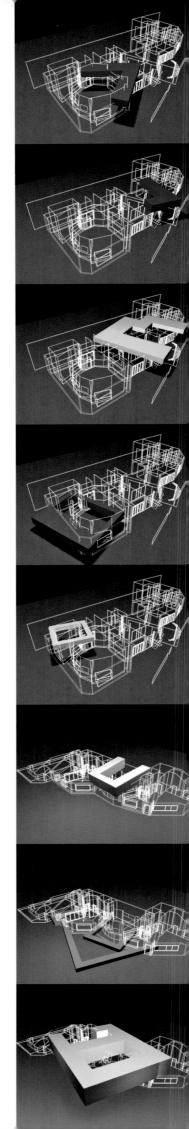

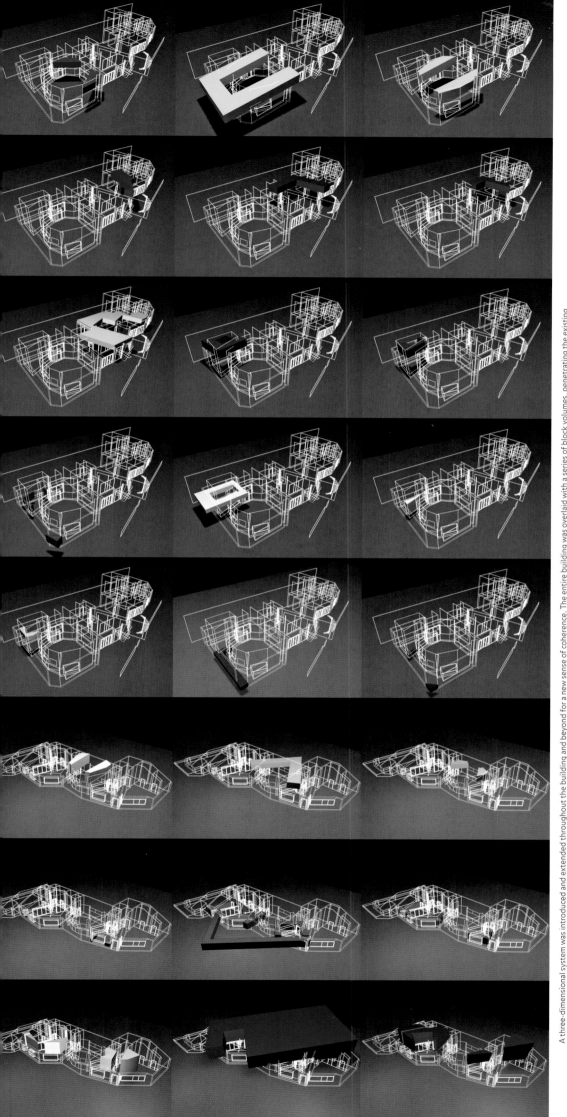

A three-dimensional system was introduced and extended throughout the building and beyond for a new sense of coherence. The entire building was overlaid with a series of block volumes, penetrating the existing and new rooms and extending beyond the shell. Generated from existing conditions and acoustic parameters in critical rooms, the volumes were positioned and then cut away where not needed. Individual volumes reappear on both floors and the exterior, suffusing the pragmatic shapes of the existing building with a new ordering system without greater changes in its shape.

01-02

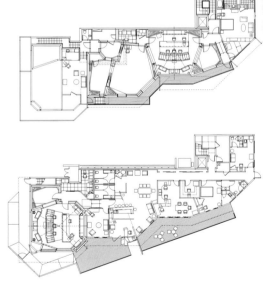

03

Mix Room A (top, center) is set up mainly for mixing and overdubs, while Control Room B (bottom) is geared towards live tracking, but both have similar dimensions and equipment. In the Isolation Booth A (right), soffit volumes converge to form an acoustical and architectural composition.

04

NO LIMIT STUDIOS
Baton Rouge, Louisiana, 1999

This complete studio facility for a major rap music label was designed to fit into an existing shell, originally laid out for a different project. Four production rooms and a film screening theater surround a large tracking studio suite.

To increase the insufficient ceiling height in the main space, a floating shell was planned below, between and around the roof trusses. Although structurally demanding, the staggered-ceiling concept allowed a greater room volume and height, and determined the look of the space. The resulting cassette-shaped ceiling is penetrated and overlaid by soft, sound-absorbing volumes acting as bass traps. The intersecting geometries of the staggered isolation shell versus the inclined volumes of the acoustic treatment form an alternating pattern at the room's ceiling boundaries. An additional geometric layer is superimposed by the arrangement and placement of the acoustic surface treatment.

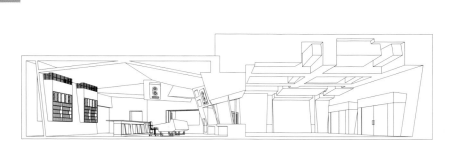

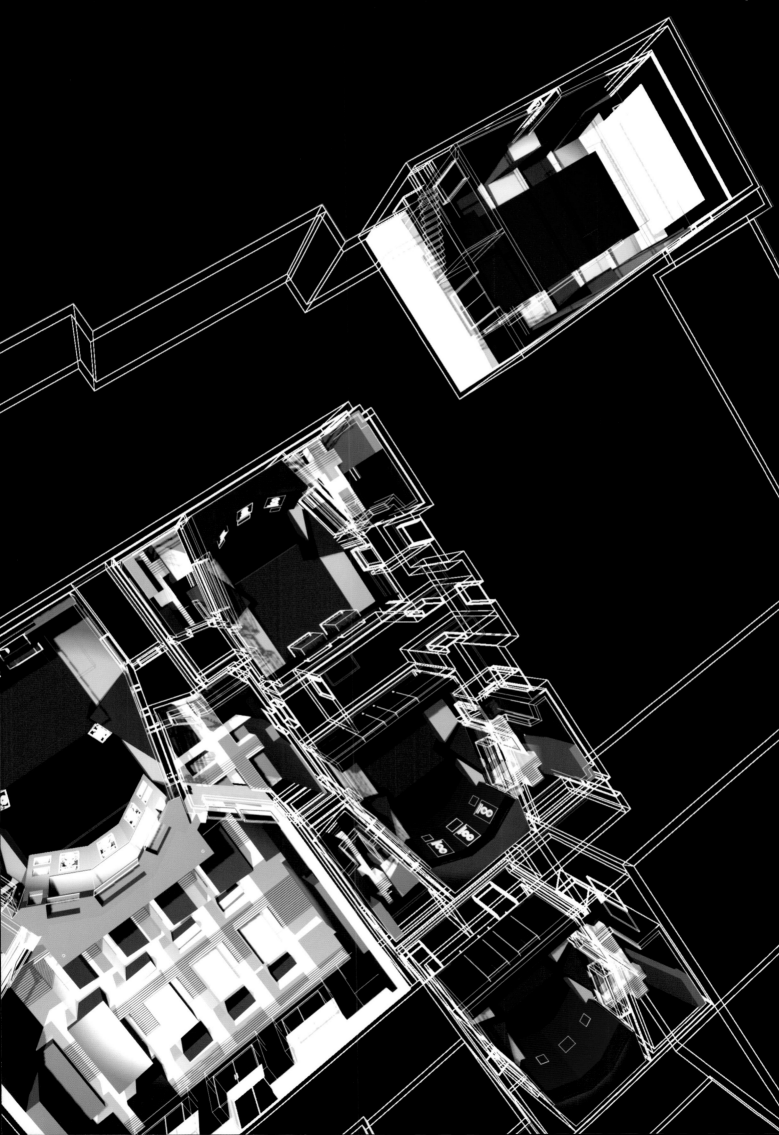

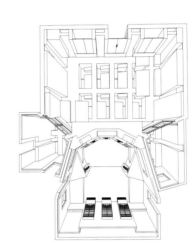

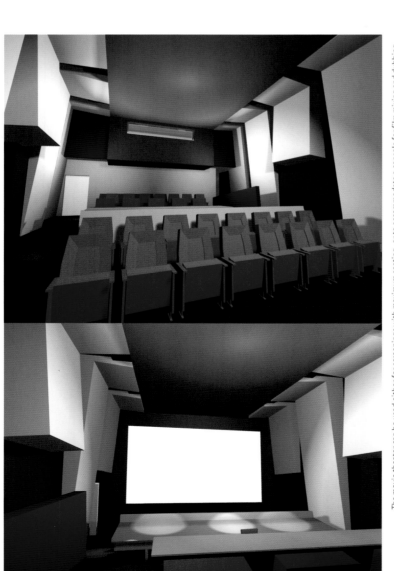

The movie theater can be used either for screenings with maximum seating, or to accommodate a console for film mixing and dubbing.

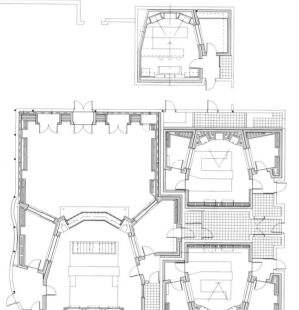

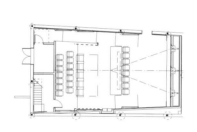

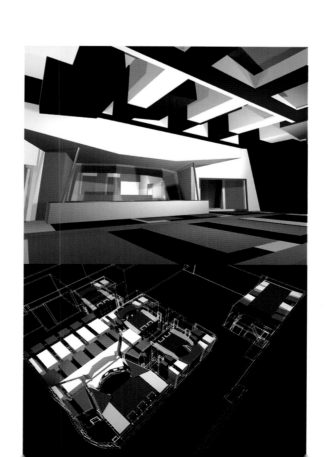

The music by Richard and Johann Strauss, Gyorgy Ligeti and Aram Khachaturian and the cinematic images in Stanley Kubrick's classic movie 2001 – A Space Odyssey have become inseparably linked in our collective cultural memory.

FILM TV VIDEO BROADCAST

The interaction of sound with architectural space is the pivotal element where music and sounds are made and assembled. The acoustic effect of the space and the boundaries it imposes upon the sound itself are a crucial yet invisible (and ideally unnoticeable) phenomenon. The eyes, often indifferently, notice the visible environment, while the ears concentrate on the all-important sound.

A second, different focus emerges when the sonic elements are only one element in a combination of media, or where the main purpose is to create visual images. The acoustic performance of these spaces still remains critical, but the optical aspects of the environment retreat further in favor of the artificial images.

The visible permanence of solid construction is now replaced by the fleeting nature of images in the making. The building's own function is no more that of a black box, visually neutral, and more a backdrop than a space to be experienced in its own right. Examples of this pure and strictly functional conception of spaces for mixed-media production can certainly be found.

But to anyone entering a movie theater, the space itself is part of the anticipation of the experience to follow. Any intrusion of the real world during the actual performance would be distracting and undesirable, neglecting the suspension of disbelief that is the prerequisite of the event. But the lights eventually go on again, the dream world is replaced by day-to-day reality, and the audience finds itself in a real spatial situation.

Sounds are by their very nature ephemeral and transitory, and do not have the solid appearance we expect of most buildings and architecture. Music, even music created artificially and played in an unnatural environment, can still credibly coexist with its physical surroundings. But for images to capture our full attention, the competing visual information in the environment needs to recede.

The following projects give a few examples of possible spaces for audiovisual production. Their crucial shared purpose is to match and merge visual and sonic information and create true multimedia content. They are all workplaces, although some of them can and do easily double as spaces for the presentation and enjoyment of the final product. In all cases there is an attempt to strike a balance between a neutral black-box approach and the investment of these spaces with a personality and visual identity of their own.

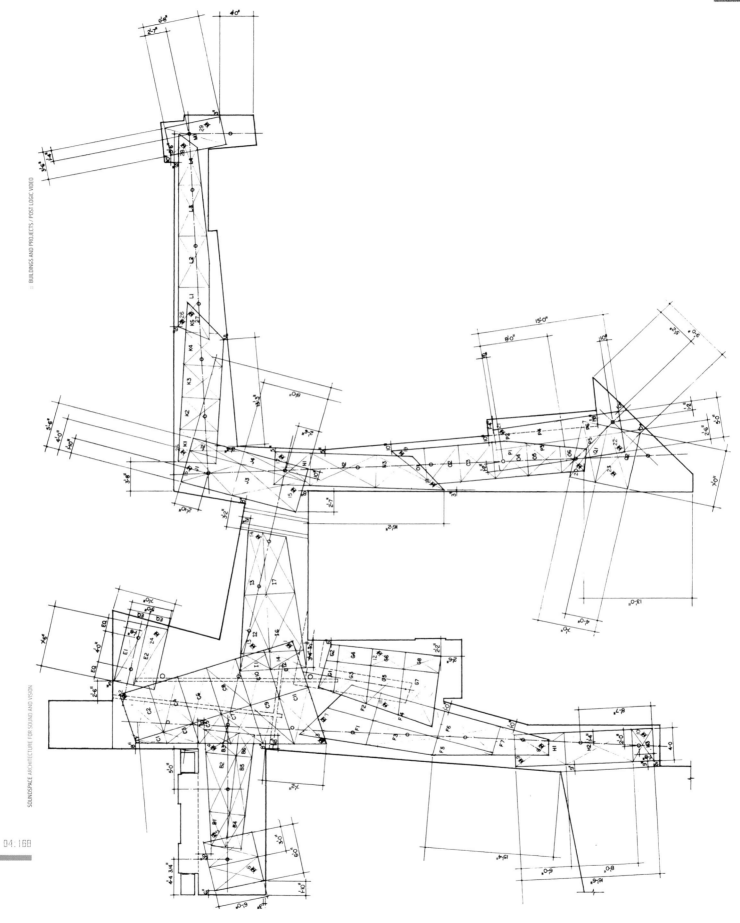

POST LOGIC VIDEO
Hollywood, California, 1992

Not primarily intended for sound, but as a video editing and film transfer facility, this project is part of a comprehensive post-production company. The goal of the design was to introduce a new architectural approach to the facility, and to set a precedent for future expansions and the imminent remodeling of the remaining existing studios.

The common entrance and reception area for the company floor had to give visitors an immediate sense of the firm's cutting-edge approach to client service and of the technical capabilities of its staff and equipment.

Suspended wood panels in the hallways unify the new part of the facility. The long shard-like shapes enliven the hallways, adding interest to the long, linear spaces, while the square panels at the ends terminate the halls. The staggered overhead landscape of white-stained maple with metal dividers extends throughout the entire project.

Two on-line video-editing bays and two telecine rooms, where film material is transferred to digital video formats, line the halls to the side.

A video graphics room occupies a skewed box at the entry and hinges the circulation flow. The outside of the room is clad in red Finply, hinting at the function of the room, where unlimited manipulations of digital images are possible.

The edit bays, similar in form and material to the telecine rooms, feature windows facing the main machine room across the hallway. To ensure privacy when needed, and to allow a more open feeling or a glance at the equipment in the machine room, an electronically induced translucent glass was used here. Controlled by an electrical switch, the glass can be changed instantaneously from a clear to a frosted pane.

01

A quarter-segment of an octagonal floor plan, the space required a thorough investigation of layout options. The central machine room houses advanced video and computer equipment, wired to every room in the project. To expose this brain of the facility, the equipment is displayed behind a custom-designed glass curtain wall around which the main hallways wrap.

01-02

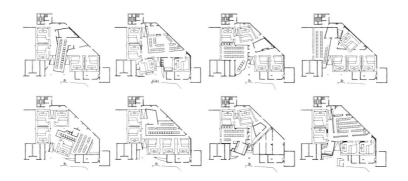

03

The "flying" beams over the entry form a gateway to the facility and provide structural support for the glass panes enclosing a small waiting area. As first conceived, they were supposed to carry a sliding glass door, later deleted. The glass is layered: broken tempered glass is sandwiched between plate glass. The break lines are emphasized by halogen spotlights, and sparkle in the otherwise calm space. The front of the reception desk is clad with corrugated glass panels.

NEWMAN SCORING STAGE
20th Century Fox, Century City, California, 1997

With the addition of a new control room and concurrent major remodel of the newly named Newman Scoring Stage, 20th Century Fox has regained its position as a premier studio film scoring facility in Los Angeles. The first sessions in the new facility included the score for the animated feature film *Anastasia*, and a re-recording of the traditional Fox Fanfare theme.

The unusually large size of the control room and its adjacent historic scoring stage are emphasized further through the use of large windows, modern materials, and a supreme sound system and acoustic environment. The 7,500-square-foot open space was originally built in 1928 as a shooting stage for Fox MovieTone Pictures and converted to a scoring stage a few years later. The original control booth was located on the second floor until 1975, when a control room was built inside the stage, taking up nearly a third of the room.

The purpose of the new project was to reclaim the lost area on the stage, and to build a control room that would be appropriate for contemporary needs of users and equipment. The control room had to live up to the sonic quality of the stage itself, which needed to maintain or even improve its acclaimed acoustics.

The large window, made possible by cutting through two massive concrete sound isolation walls, allows a complete view of the stage. The front wall around the window is clad in sound absorbing sintered aluminum panels.

The stage itself, dedicated in honor of past Fox Music Directors Alfred and Lionel Newman, is now brought back to its original size. The new east wall of the stage complements the original three walls, and further enhances the acoustical and visual properties of the stage. The new wall features dramatic geometric shapes clad in maple panels, concrete diffusor blocks, and includes talkback speakers and a film projection window. The restored hard rock maple floor, microphone panels and a new DC lighting system complete the remodel.

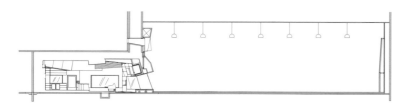

The 1,500-square-foot control room houses a tracking and mixing console 23 feet wide with a large 5-channel monitoring system. Despite its size, which can accommodate thirty or more people without distracting the mixers and engineers, the room feels comfortable and intimate.

04–05

The main recording space accommodates over 125 musicians in a scoring setup. New wall treatments recall the old zigzag plywood walls of the original stage, left untouched on three sides. Additional isolation booths were planned for the far corners (model, above left) but never built.

01

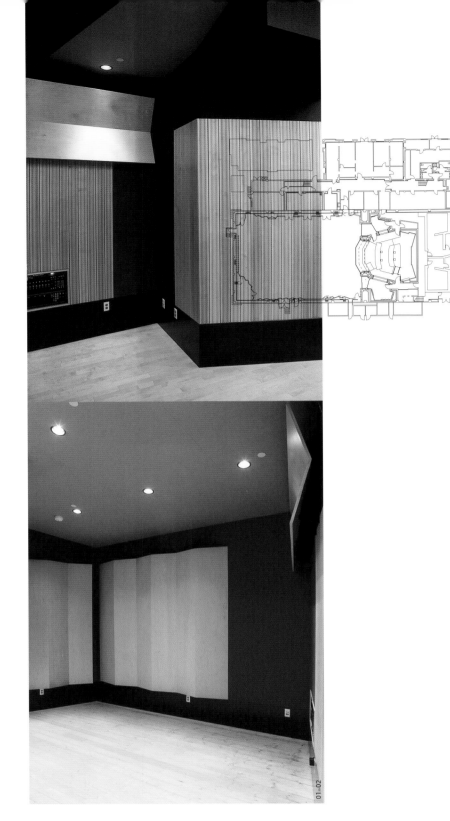

01—02

03

04

Isolation booths for vocals and drums were added to both sides of the control room. Maple zigzag panels and diffusor strips control sound reflections. Varied room sizes allow acoustic flexibility.

ASYMMETRICAL STUDIO
Hollywood, California, 1997

SOUNDSPACE ARCHITECTURE FOR SOUND AND VISION

The owner of this project, an independent film director, contributed greatly to the inspiration for the building. The design was informed by a fascination with his work, not only films and television, but also music, paintings, lyrics, cartoons and furniture designs.

Parallels between the architectural design process and methods used during movie shooting became apparent, and were exploited. For example, a new setback line at the northwest corner did not allow the addition to line up with the lower floor. This restriction led to the generation of further angled cuts into the volume of the theater. Their seeming randomness reflects the idiosyncratic nature of the owner's work, while accommodating an initially problematic zoning situation. Similar responses, where obstacles are ultimately turned into benefits, can also be seen in the owner's filmmaking. Before demolition started, the house had been a set for his last film, where it played a starring role as the scene of an unfolding schizophrenic and chaotic tale. Trace elements of the movie's themes remain, both physically and, more subtly, in a similar approach to problem-solving and design.

The project is a remodel and addition to a small 1950s house on a steep uphill slope. The program includes a movie screening room (also to be used for sound design, editing and music recording) and a painting and drawing studio. A small office on the lower floor, a kitchen and an outdoor patio above the roof level were also added.

The two main spaces can be seen as opposite extremes within a common shell. While the painting studio needs natural and diffused light, the screening room requires complete darkness. The openness of the painting space contrasts with the absolute enclosure of the recording studio.

The painting and drawing room relies on a connection with the real outside world, whereas the virtual reality of the film and sound production in the other spaces demand perfect isolation and seclusion. The natural light coming through the skylights and windows contrasts with the artificial projection rays through the celluloid. Street noises and birdsong are audible in the painting studio, but are excluded and replaced in the screening theater by man-made sounds produced by amplifiers and loudspeakers. Likewise, traditional manual methods of oil painting and chalk drawing on the one hand must coexist with the newest digital sound and picture technology on the other.

In short, two divergent spatial concepts are combined, contrasting with and influencing each other. The typically Californian dissolution of the boundaries between inside and outside is confronted by the secluded dreamworld of a virtual reality. The exterior of the building reflects the duality of the inside, but mediates between the two different aspects to create a dynamic, if tense, equilibrium.

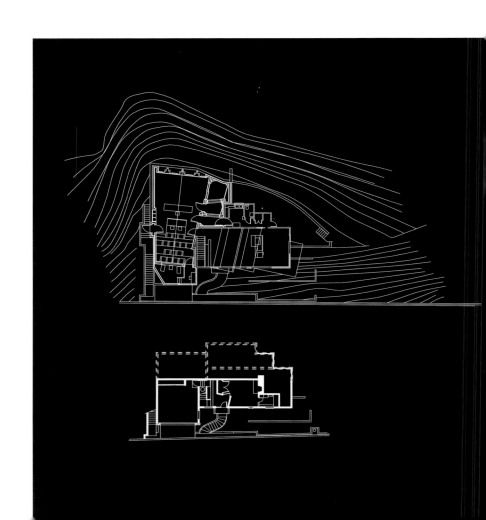

The cuts into the theater volume and the protruding shapes of the skylights balance the disparate masses. The gray monolithic skin (at first conceived as partially red) contributes to the effect. The orientation of the skylights and the shape of the theater create an overlying grid that plays off of the existing structure.

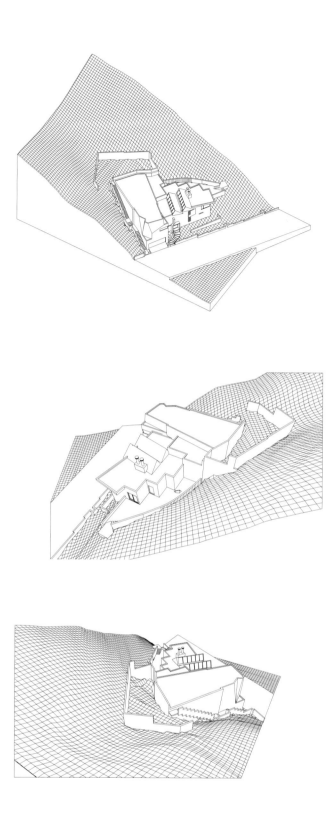

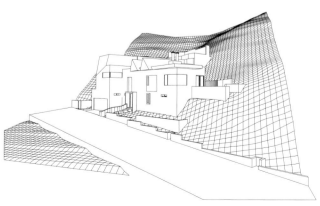

The theater's Finply wall paneling, custom wood diffusor strips, gray wall fabrics (used with the reverse side out) and red velvet curtains create an intimate environment. The fixed seating is custom-designed and built.

The theater is built deep into the hill. Putting the film screen and loudspeaker system against the massive retaining wall anchors them solidly, and backs the sound energy and visual illusions with a mass of bedrock.

01

02

03–05

SOUNDSPACE ARCHITECTURE FOR SOUND AND VISION

SOUNDSPACE ARCHITECTURE FOR SOUND AND VISION

01–02

The painting studio is opened up by two large north-facing skylights. Extending out over the west façade, they spill light from the interior down to the street at night. The space is almost doubled in height by the skylights, and washed in diffuse natural light.

03

CHRISTOPHE BECK STUDIO
Santa Monica, California, 2000

This small music writing and recording studio occupies a brick warehouse space in a light-industrial area. Designed for a successful composer, the facility serves as a personal workspace for film and television soundtracks.

The architectural concept has a dual focus: to utilize and guide the available natural light and to arrange the enclosed rooms inside the building envelope as a three-dimensional landscape. Thus, the positive volumes are stacked for spatial effect and natural circulation flow, while the remaining negative space of the open areas is itself carefully shaped. Thanks to existing openings in the roof and walls, daylight is guided around and into the building blocks of the program. The composition of the volumes and spaces reinforces the natural light and increases the spatial interest and complexity with very few and limited elements.

The sound lock, the pivotal element in the spatial arrangement, accesses the main studio spaces and blocks direct sound transmission from the common areas and between studios. Its glass cube serves as the focal point for the negative space and common areas around the stacked volumes. The access ramp leads up to the lounge, but is transformed from a pure circulation area into a habitable space. The tilted wall of the main control room is acoustically derived, but opens up the ramp space. Galvanized metal sheathing, raw steel, painted concrete floors and glass evoke the space's industrial heritage.

Inside the studio the rooms are more refined, responding to the acoustical needs and comfort level desired during long sessions. The small but crucial recording space is placed in the center of the closed spaces. Acoustically isolated, it receives natural light through its skylight, windows and glazed door. Axial symmetry, frequency response, and a large reflection-free zone determine the layout of the main control room. This room is positioned to take advantage of two symmetrically placed skylights in the rear, which are then matched with more glass in its isolation shell.

Research into the owner's working methods and use of equipment, along with adherence to his strict ergonomic guidelines, has produced moveable video monitors, equipment racks and keyboards. Arranged for maximum flexibility, the equipment furniture, shelves and racks are custom-designed to fit the space and the specific circumstances of the program.

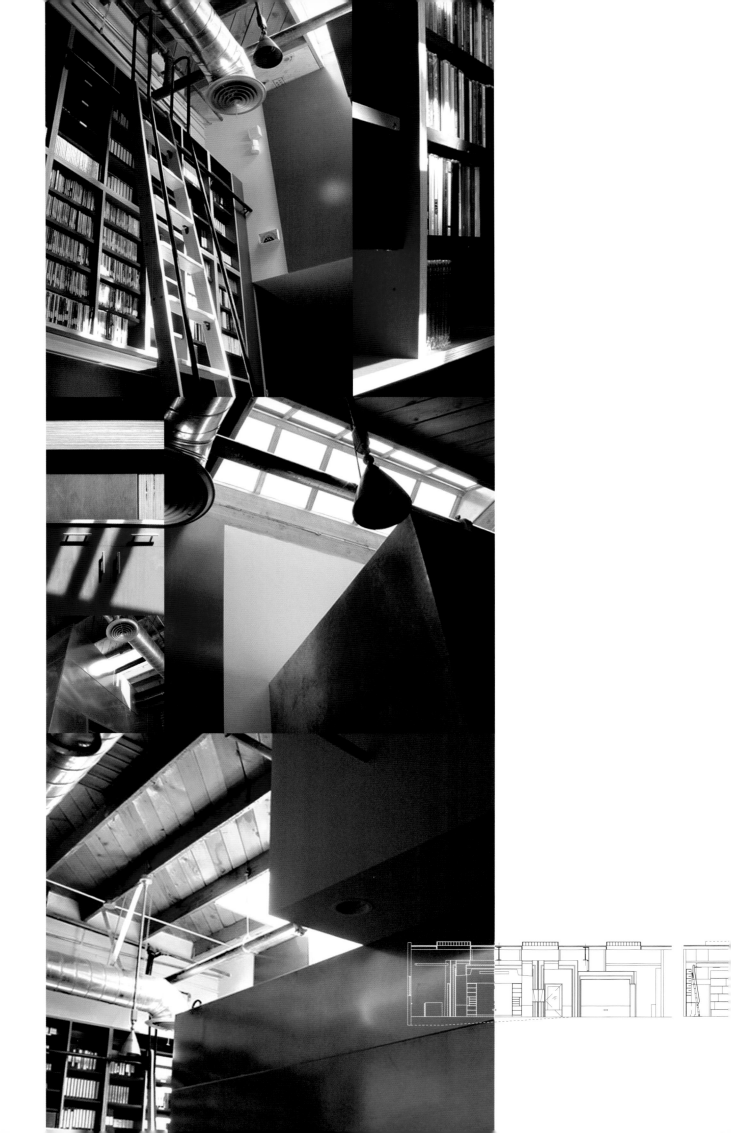

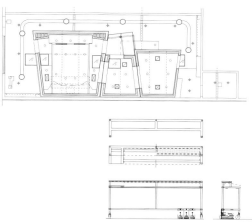

01-02

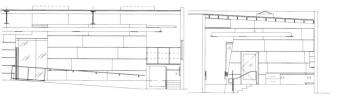

NATIONAL PUBLIC RADIO
Culver City, California, 2002

Public radio provides a welcome alternative to the advertisement-driven commercial stations in the United States, and with in-depth reporting and intelligent programming, it is favored by a large audience. An authoritative source of reliable news and journalistic excellence, its stations also regularly feature arts and entertainment programs.

National Public Radio is the largest provider of content to hundreds of stations throughout the nation, with contributions from a worldwide staff of over seven hundred. Reporters are stationed in domestic and international bureaus, supported by their headquarters in Washington, D.C.

After over thirty years of operations, the importance of providing news from the western United States and the need for a major back-up facility away from the capital led to the instigation of a West Coast expansion facility in the Los Angeles area. The collapse of the Internet boom had left a supply of nicely built-out but abandoned buildings in the area, with technical and communications systems already in place. One such building, under a double bow-truss roof, was chosen for the new production facility, and is projected to accommodate ninety people when fully operational.

While the basic infrastructure and the general areas were perfectly suited to the planned facility, the studios needed to be rebuilt to fulfill the demands of audio recording and on-air broadcasting. Five production booths supplement the two new main broadcast studios with their own control rooms. A high level of sound insulation for the studio shells was the basic requirement, along with an acoustic environment suitable for radio production.

Room-acoustic parameters were addressed with a mix of absorptive foam panels used previously in the facility, recycled cotton fabric pads, and expanded polypropylene panels; this avoided using costly fabric surfaces.

An elaborate data network connects all rooms to central servers and to the Washington facility via satellite and fiber optics, so allowing for redundant operation from both locations.

TF1 TRUCK

Paris, France, 1997

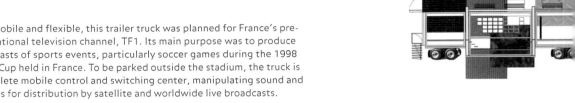

Both mobile and flexible, this trailer truck was planned for France's premier national television channel, TF1. Its main purpose was to produce broadcasts of sports events, particularly soccer games during the 1998 World Cup held in France. To be parked outside the stadium, the truck is a complete mobile control and switching center, manipulating sound and pictures for distribution by satellite and worldwide live broadcasts.

While able to travel normally between broadcasts, the truck unfolds when prepared for use as a studio.

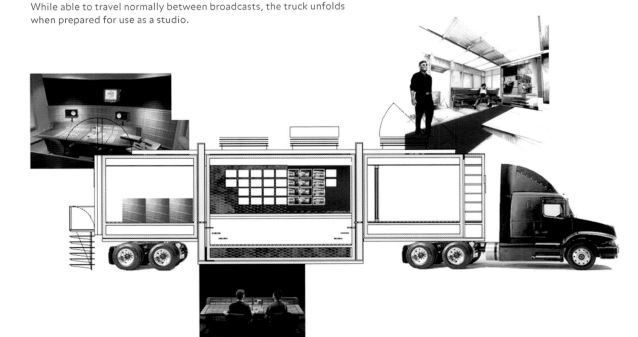

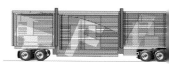

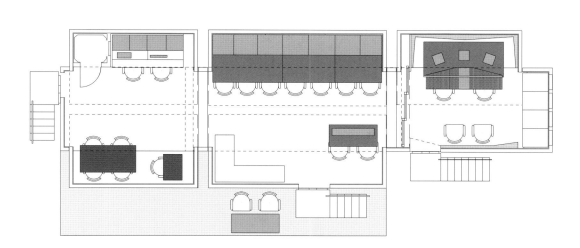

There is plenty of equipment at the [...] school, and like any good technically oriented school, it keeps changing to keep up with the times. But there is plenty of music training, too, which appeals to me because I'm one of those old-fashioned types who thinks that musicians make the best audio professionals. The product of our industry is music — technology is merely the delivery system.   PAUL D. LEHRMAN

EDUCATIONAL FACILITIES

The growing need for new entertainment content is fueling the demand for knowledgeable professionals familiar with media production processes and skilled in the operation of current equipment.

As the music industry grapples with changes in distribution patterns and digital technology, production methods are evolving as well, and there is a continual need for new skills. The film and television industries rely on producers, technicians and engineers working behind the scenes to complete pre- and post-production for images and sounds. The growth of delivery channels for traditional media, from broadcast to cable and satellite, only adds to the demand for more processing of the media content.

In addition to new releases, existing movies and records are being reprocessed for new consumer formats. In the audio world, old and new records are being remastered for surround-sound playback. Movies are redone for videotape and DVDs, edited for various markets, dubbed for foreign languages, and generally manipulated. Actual filming in digital formats – like sophisticated new special-effects and animation techniques – is a technology-intensive process. Recent additions to established formats, like computer games and Internet-based content, also contribute to the need for computer-literate media-production graduates.

As a result of the continued growth in all these fields, both public and private educational institutions are vying to fulfill demand for the appropriate education. A recent count in trade-magazine directories showed more than 120 different schools for audio production in North America alone.

Universities and colleges offer Bachelor's degrees, while trade schools have programs as short as twelve to sixteen months. Different programs focus on audio production, post-production, film, television and radio, game design, and much more, in any conceivable combination. While most longer college degree courses incorporate subjects such as music or engineering, the trade schools mainly focus on hands-on practical training.

Developments in technology that have made equipment more affordable and easier to use have also brought the creative and production processes closer together. It is now possible for musicians to engineer their own music, and a background in media technology is very useful for many more people.

Whether students come from a music background or are more interested in the technology, they all seem to share a deep enthusiasm for the field they are about to enter. School facilities dedicated to the teaching of media production have to provide the students and faculty with real-life situations and state-of-the-art equipment. At the same time the educational environment must foster the natural passion of students and continue to nurture their initial excitement.

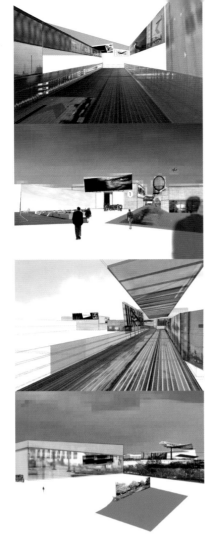

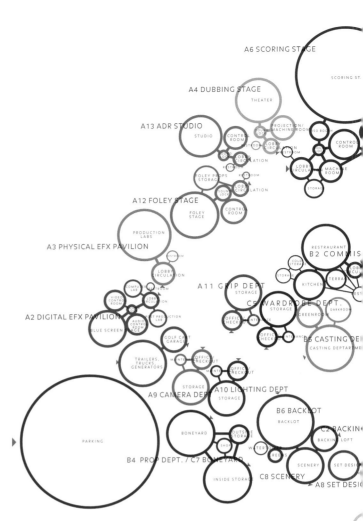

A6 SCORING STAGE

SCORING ST.

A4 DUBBING STAGE

THEATER

A13 ADR STUDIO

PROJECTION/MACHINE ROOM

STUDIO · CONTROL ROOM · CONTROL ROOM

A12 FOLEY STAGE

FOLEY PROPS STORAGE · FOLEY STAGE · CONTROL ROOM

A3 PHYSICAL EFX PAVILION

RESTAURANT
B2 COMMIS

A11 GRIP DEPT · STORAGE

C5 WARDROBE DEPT.

A2 DIGITAL EFX PAVILION

BLUE SCREEN · AUDIO CONTROL ROOM

GOLF CART GARAGE

B5 CASTING DE

TRAILERS TRUCKS GENERATORS · OFFICE CHECKOUT

A9 CAMERA DEPT · A10 LIGHTING DEPT · STORAGE

B6 BACKLOT · BACKLOT

C2 BACKIN

PARKING

BONEYARD · OUTSIDE STORAGE

B4 PROP DEPT. / C7 BONEYARD · INSIDE STORAGE · C8 SCENERY

SCENERY · SET DESI

A8 SET DESI

FULL SAIL CAMPUS

Winter Park, Florida, 2001

Full Sail Real World Education is a college for media production that offers programs in the recording arts, film and video production, digital media, game design, show production and computer animation. This private institution near the University of Central Florida has experienced rapid growth, and is on the verge of another significant increase of the student body. The enrollment has risen from about 2,300 to over 4,000 students within a period of only two years, and the curriculum is still being expanded to incorporate additional programs.

As a result, several possibilities for the future needs of the institution are being investigated simultaneously. The campus, in Orlando, is centered around a two-story zigzag building in an office park. The growth of the curriculum has already led to expansion into a newly acquired adjacent shopping mall complex.

Plans for the expansion of the movie school, including a Hollywood-style film lot on a 14-acre property across the street are also being considered. Providing studies in all aspects of film production, the school needs a campus duplicating the reality of real-life commercial production facilities. The expected size of this additional facility is around 300,000 square feet, and includes sound stages, dubbing theaters, production labs and studios, as well as a back lot and other outdoor filming areas.

One main purpose of this master plan is to connect the various school departments through a series of bridges and pedestrian ways, and to reorganize the vehicular traffic and parking concept. To improve circulation and the efficiency of potential synergistic relationships, the placement of the various program parts is being analyzed and questioned.

By creating an overall architectural image for the institution, the plan tries to integrate the dissimilar buildings within the growing campus into a coherent and continuous fabric of structures and exterior connections. Welcoming and memorable outdoor spaces linking the buildings strive for an educational environment that nurtures learning and interaction between students and faculty.

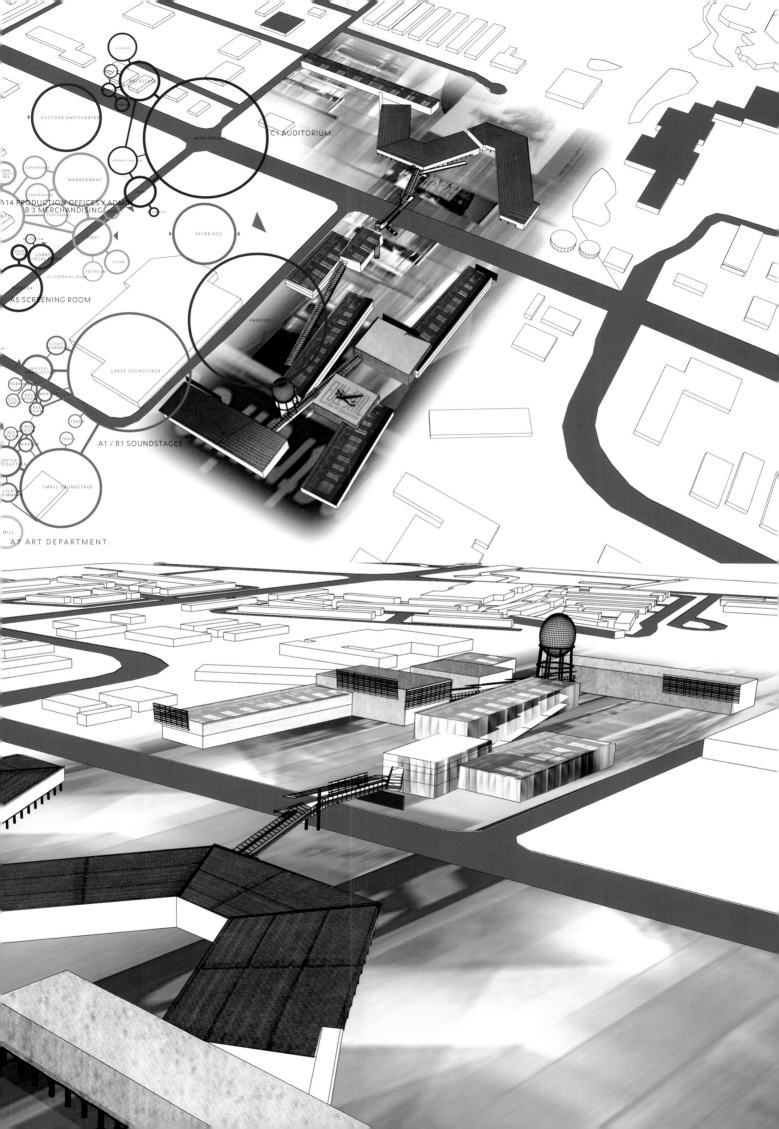

OUTDOOR AMPITHEATER

SUPPORT
BACKSTAGE
STAFF

MANAGEMENT

CONFERENCE

ADMINISTRATION

COMM
CULTURE
AREA

CONFERENCE

A14 PRODUCTION OFFICES X ADMIN
B 3 MERCHANDISING

AUDITORIUM

C1 AUDITORIUM

CONFERENCE

LOBBY

SKYBRIDGE

STORE

SOUND
LOCK

LOBBY
CIRCULATION

RESTROOM

A5 SCREENING ROOM

THEATER

A5 SCREENING ROOM

PARKING

LIGHT
DIMMER

OFFICE/
PRODUCTION

PARKING

LARGE SOUNDSTAGE

REST
ROOM

GOLF
CART

MAKE
UP
ROOM

GREEN
ROOM

TRASH

REST
ROOM

MAKEUP

TRASH

A1 / B1 SOUNDSTAGES

OFFICE/
PRODUCTION

LIGHT
DIMMER

SMALL SOUNDSTAGE

MILL

A7 ART DEPARTMENT

FULL SAIL DUBBING THEATER
Winter Park, Florida, 2003

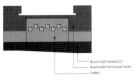

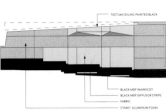

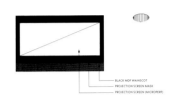

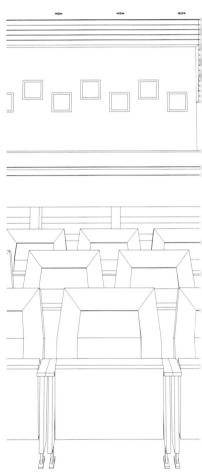

As part of the college's reorganization and improvement a film dubbing theater is being inserted into the existing main school building. The project is the signature facility and anchor for the film production program, which is experiencing a particularly strong surge. The architecture is focused on the theme of film, its production, spirit and enjoyment.

The lobby, the centerpiece of the project, is a two-story open space dedicated to the experience of and immersion into the world of filmmaking and film watching. With its architectural elements and multimedia effects the space provides a glimpse of the ephemeral nature of movies. Constant movement through the space, changing perspectives, lights and shadows, colors and contrasts, reflections, multiple layers and shifting perceptions are utilized, and finally overlaid with moving images borrowed from the history of film itself.

The actual film dubbing lab is the destination beyond the lobby, and holds an audio-for-film mixing console, editing booths, and an array of comfortable seats for movie screenings. Foamed open-cell aluminum panels on the walls create an acoustically and visually stimulating, almost science-fiction environment. But once the lights are down, the main focus is the thirty-foot-wide screen and the sound generated by a powerful surround-sound speaker system. Sound processing is a crucial step in contemporary film post-production and this facility will allow school graduates to become familiar with the ultimate environment for that purpose.

Complementing the hands-on aspects of teaching movie production, the spaces capture the excitement and imagination generated by the medium, both motivating the current students and enticing prospective ones to enroll.

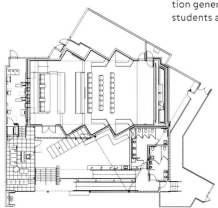

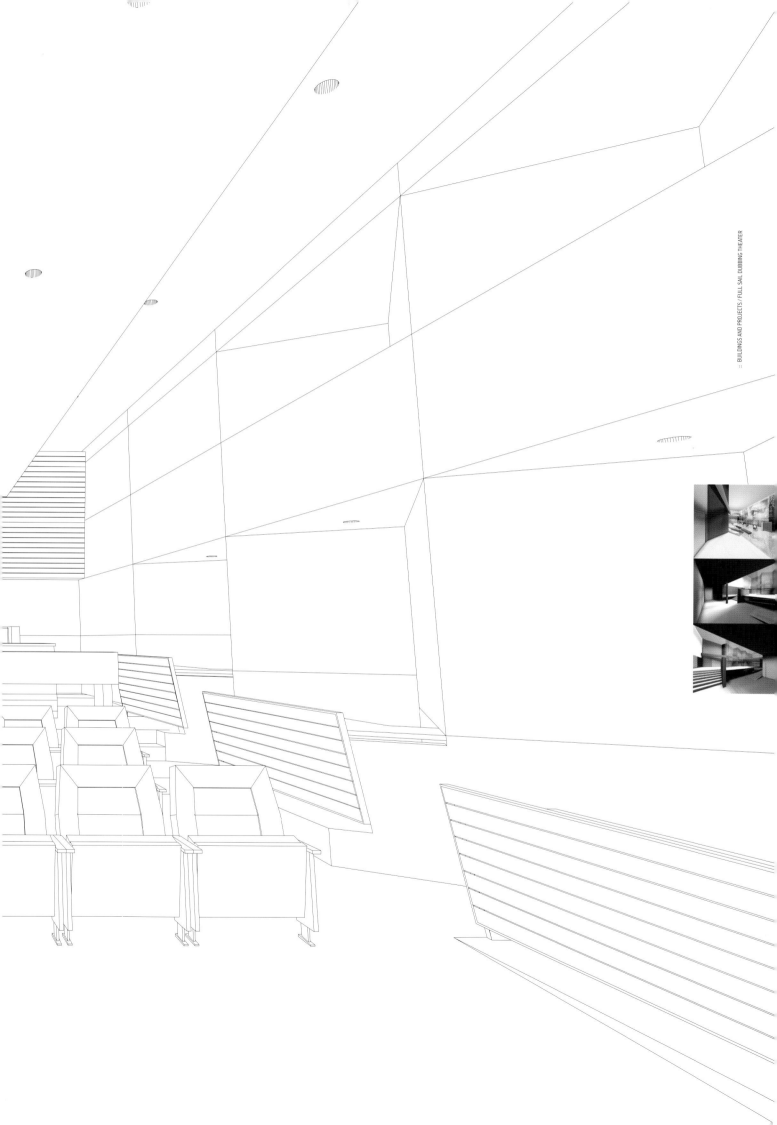

A large glass screen takes up one side of the lobby, with oversized random film projections visible from both sides. Doubling as guardrail and divider for the requisite ramp, it is the main sculptural element in the space. Other multimedia events can use flat-screen monitors, and a glass projection floor, centered on the raised lobby floor. The equipment and computer room is visible through a Profilit glass curtain wall off the lobby, exposing the technological aspects of filmmaking. An abstract movie-house marquee is constructed from the same linear glass profiles, and strong lighting through multiple material layers suggests looking into projector beams and klieg lights.

Large prints on the walls evoke the history of both black-and-white and color films, and constitute additional visual layers behind moving projections and lighting. A bar and built-in seats are practical elements in the media-saturated environment. An enclosed mezzanine off the lobby lets observers look down into the adjacent dubbing lab, and into the lobby. Floating above the lobby, the mezzanine lounge is clad in aluminum foam panels with an irregular yet shiny surface.

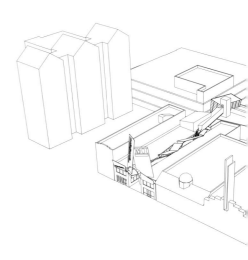

01-02

MUSICIANS INSTITUTE

Hollywood, California, 1997

The first completed project in a string of collaborations with the music and entertainment industry school was a recording studio for the audio engineering program. While functionally equal to a professional studio, the room's finishes are brighter than in a typical commercial facility, inspired as they are by the youthful optimism and energy of the students. The open and generous layout permits easy teaching and learning in groups gathered around the equipment.

In 1997, after the acquisition of another building adjacent to the school, and concurrently with the planning of a television studio for UTB TV there, a master plan for the complex was developed. This plan and architectural concept attempts to connect and unify an unrelated cluster of buildings into a coherent campus for the school and its affiliated partners.

The project shifts the main access point to the campus from side streets to the more prominent Hollywood Boulevard, and infuses that area with visitor-friendly uses, while greatly increasing the visibility of the school. The newly conceived elements take their inspiration from the eclectic pedestrian mix on the sidewalks, with their famous inlaid stars, and from the main function of the building as a school of rock 'n' roll.

The backbone and signature piece of the campus is a new pedestrian bridge, providing access and a recognizable approach to the different areas of the school. Straddling an alley, which now separates the school into two parts, the bridge unifies the campus. A "sky lobby" at the south end of the bridge overlooks the facility while offering a view over the roofs of the neighborhood to the hills in the distance.

In addition to the television station, the former "Panavision" building contains a rehearsal stage and classrooms for the acting school. Its eastern part is the main circulation node in the complex and the connecting point between the various structures.

The courtyard building on Hollywood Boulevard includes a new coffeehouse and serves as the new main entrance to the MI campus. Other planned uses include a gift shop, a reception area to connect the school with the public, and an outdoor stage for live performances in the courtyard.

The vitality of the location and the program are reflected in the dynamic shapes and arrangement of the new parts. The project serves as the catalyst for the transformation and opening up to the public of this established institution, which blends in perfectly with the culture and atmosphere of its surroundings.

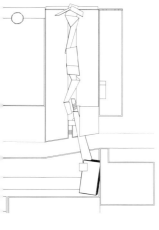

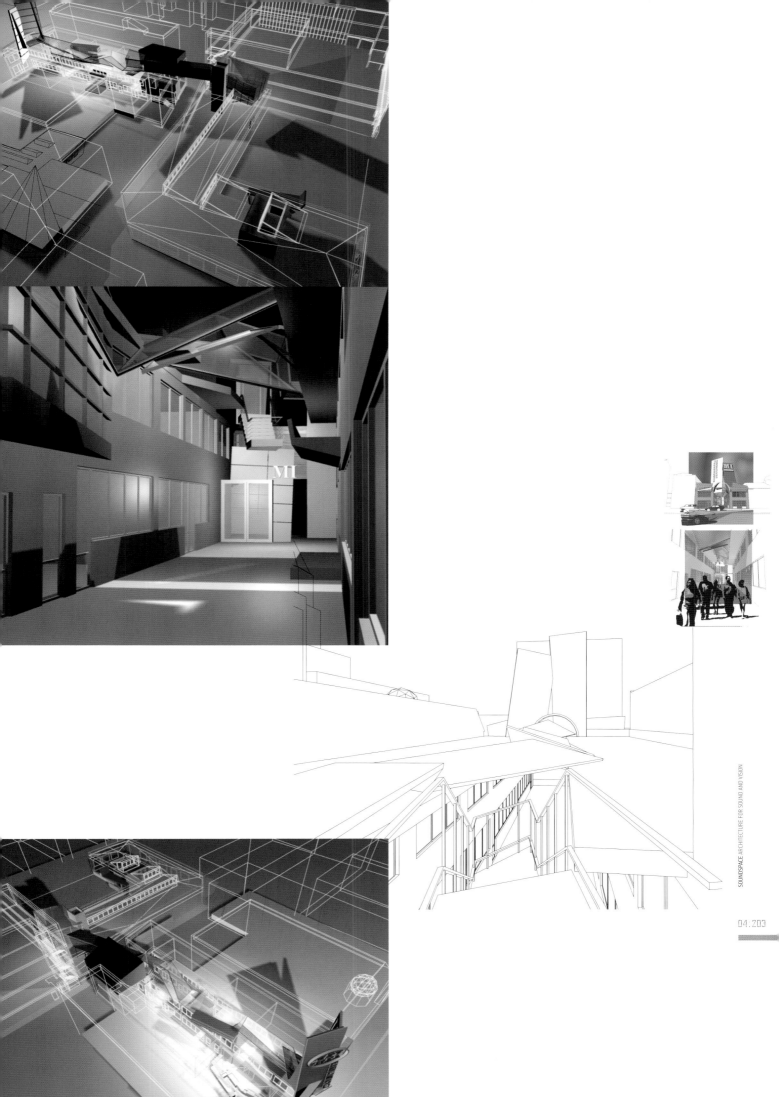

CENTER FOR THE RECORDING ARTS
North Hollywood, California, 2003

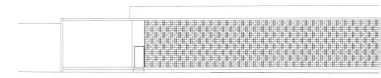

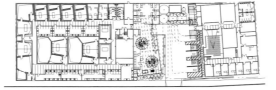

In 1994 the Los Angeles Recording Workshop built a new school facility in a former bank building in North Hollywood. The main studio teaching space was designed by studio bau:ton, and served as the signature space for the school. Six years later the school site was included in a redevelopment zone by the City of Los Angeles, and another move became necessary.

Two buildings, totaling 32,000 square feet, former laboratory spaces for a health maintenance organization, were chosen for the new school, only about a mile away. The new site is adjacent to Royaltone Studios (see page 105), one of a long lineup of commercial studio facilities along Magnolia Boulevard. An existing courtyard between the two structures adjoins the street, and serves as the entry point to both buildings.

Concurrently with the move, the school's name was changed to "The Center for the Recording Arts," and the student population increased to twice its former size. The new classrooms and study labs provide an environment that mirrors the excitement of the education itself. New recording-lab spaces closely resemble the real conditions in professional studios but have been modified for the express purpose of recording instruction. The larger western building houses recording studios and computer labs, while the eastern structure is dedicated to classrooms, an auditorium and administration offices. The courtyard between the two links the buildings, serving as a recreational space, and connecting rather than separating them spatially.

A tilted glass box inserted into the courtyard hosts the student lounge, and by exposing the activities and the energy of the institution contributes to the open and relaxed feeling of the school. A canopy screen of photovoltaic solar panels is suspended over the glass box, simultaneously shading the glass and generating energy for the equipment power and the cooling needs of the buildings. Two round pods housing computer and listening stations are placed within the glass volume, accessible to students at all times for self-guided classes and study.

The architecture of the studios and common areas is relaxed and straightforward, with natural light added to the common areas, and industrial materials used for aesthetic and visual purposes.

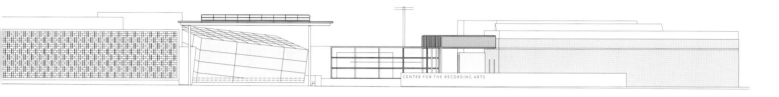

CENTER FOR THE RECORDING ARTS

A gorgeous thing is happening now as technology becomes more common. It's like years ago, when there was a piano or guitar in everyone's home and everybody would know how to use them. It's excellent, because if one's human spirit wants to write a song, it's more likely to be captured now. Good music always wins. BJÖRK

HOME STUDIOS

Composers and musicians have always enjoyed working in their own home environment, playing music in surroundings suitable to their creative taste. Writing and practicing generally posed no problems, except possibly for an unhappy neighbor or spouse who complained about the noise. From Mozart's apartment in Baroque Vienna to the suburban garages used by teenage rock bands in more recent times, music is best, and cheapest, made at home.

Other aspects of music, such as public performances or actual recording and mixing, still required outside facilities, from the concert hall to the commercial recording studio. But over the last decade or so, reductions in size and cost and the digitalization of recording equipment have fostered a migration of ever greater parts of the music production process from commercial studios to individualized home setups.

Initially fought furiously by commercial studio owners when they first emerged as a building genre, home studios have now become a ubiquitous part of urban areas like the Hollywood Hills. The use of zoning laws to shut down private studio operations was successful at first, but home studios were in effect an early form of telecommuting, and their growth was inevitable.

Usually dedicated to one single writing, recording or mixing project at a time, these facilities are now often called "project studios." But a project studio can also be part of a commercial facility, whereas here we have emphasized actual home studios, showing projects that are truly located in a residential situation.

The range of existing and envisioned future facilities varies greatly, both in regards to equipment and to physical space, and of course, to budget. Everything can be found, from a simple acoustical fix in an existing garage or spare bedroom to a full studio environment that surpasses many commercial facilities.

While technical advances have made previously exclusive equipment affordable to many, the physical space still poses the same old problems. A typical case in the Los Angeles area is the conversion of residential garages into studio spaces. The standard size of a two-car garage works fairly well for conversion to a personal studio setup. However, eliminating the covered parking spaces required by codes can lead to difficulties with the zoning authorities. When the appropriate permits are sought, the lost space has to be replaced, thereby significantly adding to the cost.

Regardless of project size, the inclusion of an actual recording space is a major factor affecting the budget of a home studio. Sound isolation is expensive, and where microphones are present the acceptable noise level is very low. In addition, the sound produced within the space should not reach the neighbors. If it does so on a regular basis, and at high levels, you have a recipe for disaster. And since musical muses can strike at three in the morning, reliance on traffic noise to cover up the emerging sound is not always sufficient.

In suburban southern California, most isolation problems concern airborne sound from one building to another. But in more urban areas, studio construction in residential structures often needs to address structure-borne noise as well, adding a whole other level of difficulty and cost.

But most importantly, home studios allow their users and owners to pursue their passion within their own walls, and to continue the age-old tradition of making music where they feel most comfortable. Whether in a rented apartment with a few hundred dollars of acoustic improvements, or in a dedicated multi-million dollar studio building next to the mansion, home studios have become an essential part of the music-production process.

STUDIO CITY, CALIFORNIA, 1999

The studio is located in an existing basement space, below the pool deck of the house it serves. Daylight and spatial clarity were major concerns for the layout. The new window overlooks the back lots and sound stages of Studio City movie studios. Finishes of light-colored wood and fabrics relate to the décor of the main house, and answer the owner's request for a workspace with a residential feel. The composing and editing room also serves as the control room for a recording booth in the front. The built-in equipment desk is on an axis with the window in the booth, and the separating sliding doors are fully glazed. [01–03]

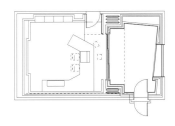

PALM BEACH, FLORIDA, 1997

An octagonal building shell had been added to this estate in South Florida, and the composing and mixing room fits tightly into its shape. Built-in main speakers follow the shape in the front, while bass traps are integrated into the back of the room, solving the acoustically problematic layout. Windows offer visual connections to the tropical landscape surrounding the house.

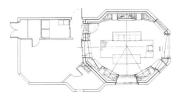

VALLEY VILLAGE, CALIFORNIA, 2002

A new double carport replaces the former garage space, now turned into a home studio with a recording booth.

HOLLYWOOD HILLS, CALIFORNIA, 1994

As befits the owner's roots in rap and heavy metal, the color scheme is completely black and red. A large window overlooks the Los Angeles Basin to the south, with the mixing console centered on it. In this control room a large shark tank occupies the acoustically sensitive rear wall. A moveable screen with diffusing wood slats can be lowered to cover the aquarium glass for critical listening situations. [04]

VIRGINIA, 2002

Owned by a successful rock band, this studio occupies
a large part of a residence and barn in rural Virginia. The
site is located on a remote wooded property, and provides
undisturbed space for rehearsals, writing and recording between tours. A large live room and two isolation booths flank
the control room. Four skylights, oriented for daylight without direct sun glare, puncture the pitched roof with its
solid lumber trusses. [01–05]

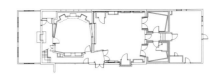

PACIFIC PALISADES, CALIFORNIA, 2001

Suspended into an existing fully glazed artist's studio, the
control room on the second floor overlooks the larger space
below. The painting studio is to be used for live recording, so
a window is extended into a glass floor, permitting sightlines
from the tracking and mixing console to the room below.

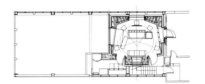

SECTION

LOS FELIZ, CALIFORNIA, 1997

Inserted into the basement of a 1910-era villa built by a silent-
movie star, the studio takes advantage of the solid and massive existing structure. A secret liquor vault, concealed behind
shelves during Prohibition, is now converted into the isolation
booth. A floating wood floor covers the undamaged original
tiles (for possible future removal) and contributes to the
soundproofing of the space from the rest of the house. [06]

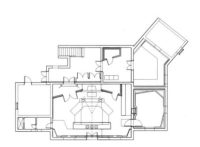

PACIFIC PALISADES, CALIFORNIA, 1995

The Pacific Palisades studio was planned for an addition to
be newly built, but with a strictly predetermined footprint.
Relative proximity of the studio rooms to neighboring homes,
and the internal connections with the main residence demanded a moderately high level of soundproofing, but no
secondary floating shell construction was deemed necessary.
An advantage of the otherwise difficult footprint is the exposure to daylight on three sides, allowing for ample window
surface. The room is entered from the house through one
of the isolation booths. [07–08]

HOLLYWOOD, CALIFORNIA, 1990

The partners' first collaborative effort, with the design predating the official founding of studio bau:ton, this project combines a residential addition with a home studio.

Removing an existing garage and replacing it with a carport freed the side yard of the property for the addition of a personal studio. An L-shaped volume forms the transition from the entrance and carport into the studio area and up to the second floor. Its open volumes step up to a platform on an intermediate level and serve as auxiliary recording spaces. The spatial development was crucial for the acoustics and the architectural sequence ascending through the space. The sectional complexity is complemented by natural light and views to the surrounding Hollywood Hills.

Tucked into the L is the piano booth, visible from the street up the long driveway. Its form is generated by acoustic parameters, with the exterior closely expressing the inside shapes and angles. With its smooth blue stucco, it creates a recognizable identity for the residence. The central composing and mix room is used for sound design, special effects and music for movies, television and high-end commercials. While no changes were made to the house itself, the carport ties together the old and new structures, and conceals the house from the street.

Double walls present a windowless façade to the closest neighbors, and structural separation prevents sound from traveling into the house.

Technology has the potential to profoundly expand the presence of art in our world, to deliver music in a series of expanding circles where creators are supported for their work and inspired to create more and greater works of art.   CARY SHERMAN

NEW MEDIA

Popular methods of sharing news, whether to entertain and enlighten or simply to express one-self, have persistently evolved over time. From cave paintings to the printing press, from smoke signals to the Internet, from wax cylinders to eight-track recorders and on to MP3 files, the history of human communication and entertainment is closely related to its cultural context.

What are now called New Media are only the latest in a continuum of ever-changing ways to convey and distribute information. But the accelerated pace of change in the age of information technology is fundamentally altering the way media, in the broadest sense, works. Changes are no longer occurring slowly over millennia, centuries or even decades; new forms follow one another in rapid succession, every few years or even every few months. Essentially different technologies are experienced by a single generation, and multiple standards and methodologies coexist side by side.

Digital technology may be the single most important current development leading to a true paradigm shift in the way data are created and experienced. One currently raging battle pitches the established record companies against proponents of free sharing of audio files on the Internet. At stake is the entire payment system for music and media creation and the copyright laws protecting artists and their representatives. The hope is that eventually a model will emerge that can ensure the freedom enjoyed thanks to the new communications systems while securing compensation for the creators and distributors of artistic content.

The term New Media defies precise definition; it covers Internet-based and streamed audio and video content, computer games, applications like picture- and sound-enabled cell phones, personal digital assistants, and a plethora of other developments. But despite its fluctuating and sometimes elusive nature, the actual creation of New Media content still depends on equipment and physical facilities, much like traditional media production. And, as in previous forms of news, art and entertainment, the substance and the methods used are in a symbiotic relationship, feeding off each other and moving things forward together.

A single laptop computer can be used to program a website, "creative" office space may serve to produce larger team projects, and entire dedicated buildings house virtual-reality labs for digital film effects or acoustically precise rooms to create surround-sound mixes. The scope and complexity of the required infrastructure is vast.

Instances of New Media facilities are described here and there throughout this book, a case in point being the authoring studios at Sony in Tokyo. Below, we present just a few examples of spaces and buildings dedicated primarily to New Media.

LIVE   TV   ONLINE

EVENT SPACE   TV BROADCAST   INTERNET

CITYSWITCH CAFE

Amsterdam – London – Berlin, 1997–2000

CitySwitch was a wide-ranging project, developed in a long collaborative process with a diverse team of multidisciplinary participants. Its primary goal was to establish a new entertainment model for the new millennium. Started in Amsterdam, based on the ideas of a young Dutch entrepreneur, the undertaking allowed the involvement of various branches of the bau:ton group affiliates, and the exploration of multiple new ideas and developments. Although it ultimately had to be abandoned, it provided invaluable insights into the workings of technology-based architectural concepts.

Essentially, the project envisages a series of nightclubs in different trend-setting European cities, all linked through high-speed broadband multimedia connections. The integrated technology allows the simultaneous experience of remote events in real time. The related group of facilities in distant cities is able to share concerts, awards programs and a wide range of other events with a mix of live action and broadcast feeds, and to interact across all the venues. Facilities for audio and video broadcasting, webcasting and live entertainment are supplemented by restaurants, café-bars and retail stores. As an extension of the dynamic possibilities of interaction on the Internet, CitySwitch would create content and broadcast it through its TV and online providers to affiliates and the public at large.

Architecturally, the clubs refer to their physical locations by using local design elements, while the group of venues is joined technologically across geographical boundaries. Simultaneously with the installation of the European Union, a fusion of local urban traditions and the global youth culture reflects the contemporary conditions of life in modern Europe. CitySwitch would break down barriers between cities, countries and cultures.

The development of a business plan and the securing of venture capital financing went along with research into the available technologies for the developing concept and with the assembly of a large project team. The technical means to achieve the stated goals were indeed available, but at a prohibitive cost, and with unacceptable limitations. As a result, investigations into cutting-edge network systems and possible technological advances were undertaken. Eventually, an ongoing collaboration with Heidelberger Engineering in Zurich was tapped for the development of a proprietary technology that could achieve the same goals more efficiently. That joint venture later inspired NET:ton engineering, which was then transformed into BridgeCo AG (see page 230).

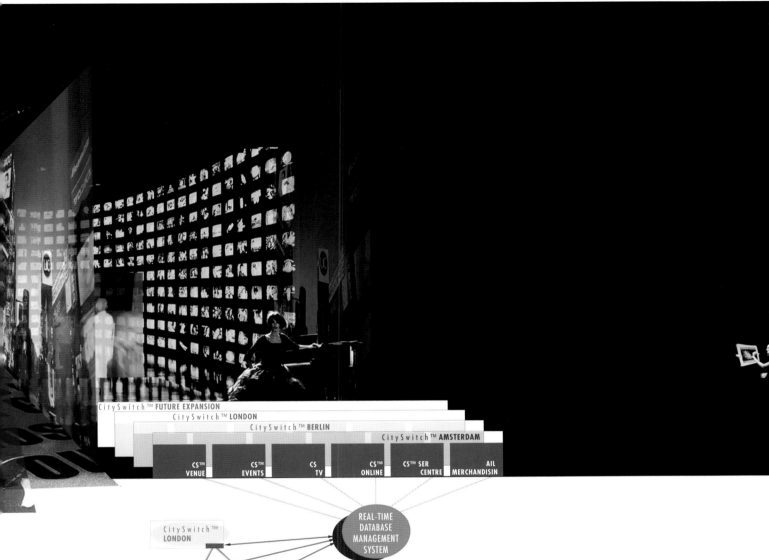

CitySwitch™ **FUTURE EXPANSION**

CitySwitch™ **LONDON**

CitySwitch™ **BERLIN**

CitySwitch™ **AMSTERDAM**

| CS™ VENUE | CS™ EVENTS | CS TV | CS™ ONLINE | CS™ SER CENTRE | AIL MERCHANDISIN |

REAL-TIME DATABASE MANAGEMENT SYSTEM

CitySwitch™ **LONDON**

CitySwitch™ **AMSTERDAM**

CitySwitch™ **BERLIN**

ENTERTAINMENT & LIVE PERFORMANCE

RESTAURANTS & CAFES

RETAIL & MERCHANDISING

TV PRODUCTION & BROADCASTING

INTERNET

SUPERTRACKS
Santa Monica, California, 2000

This small space in an existing facility was made available to house a new multi-use conference and presentation room. As a traditional meeting and teleconferencing space, the tables and chairs can be arranged in different configurations. And in its alter ego as a screening and sound presentation room, the space contains couches and comfortable seats in several rows.

Spatial constraints and the lack of storage outside the room led to the development of custom-designed and foldable furniture, which can be stored away below the screen when not in use.

A separate projection booth allows high-definition video screenings, with an integrated surround-sound system providing the soundtrack. A wired credenza inside the room serves as a setup platform for equipment brought in specifically for a testing or presentation session.

A curtain of stainless-steel mesh, which adds a metallic sheen and a pervasive sense of the high-tech environment, protects the sound-absorptive soft wall lining.

SCREENWALL

LEFT CHANNEL, SUBWOOFER, CENTER
CHANNEL AND RIGHT CHANNEL
MOUNTED BEHIND SCREEN

EQUIPMENT RACKS

CONFERENCE TABLES IN STORAGE
POSITION BELOW SCREEN

LINE OF CREDENZA SHOWN DASHED

LINE OF PROJECTOR MOUNTED IN CONTROL
ROOM SHOWN DASHED

SURROUND CHANNEL
MOUNTED @ CEILING

PROJECTOR PORT

SURROUND CHANNELS
MOUNTED @ CEILING

WINDOW TO CONTROL
ROOM

SURROUND CHANNEL
MOUNTED @ CEILING

THINKTANK
Chicago, Illinois, 2000

In the mid-1990s studio bau:ton worked with Swell Pictures in Chicago on the relocation of their facilities into a new high rise building. After the initial move, when Swell built out 20,000 square feet of video and audio post-production suites, additional audio rooms were designed and built by the team.

Encouraged by the strong growth of the Internet and the advertising industry's established presence in Chicago, Swell's owner started Thinktank, a multidisciplinary firm offering media production, in-house advertising concepts, identity development and branding, and graphic and web design.

The lease of an additional floor for the new company called for plans to construct creative office space and administrative and managerial offices. The importance of capturing the creative energy of the startup company, with its unusual full-service approach to advertising, was paramount. At the same time, empty design gestures, so familiar in the heyday of the initial Internet boom, were to be avoided in favor of comfortable and efficient work spaces.

The design combines polycarbonate-clad enclosed spaces with custom-designed open workstations. Subtly tilting wall planes are supplemented by a scale of varying transparencies of the cladding materials. Enhanced by acoustic treatment inside the rooms, the walls also serve as projection screens for video content from in-house productions. The projections, the angles, and the layering of different transparencies combine to form a complex arrangement within a straightforward basic layout.

The workstations are based on standard elements found in scaffolding construction and allow an unlimited variety of combinations and arrangements. Placed to the north of the plan, the open area allows unobstructed views of the lake from the high-rise floor.

A collaborative effort between Thinktank and studio bau:ton, this project (left) addresses the branded presence of a major computer chip manufacturer and mobile communications company within a large office-supplies retailer.

The handles of a craftsman's tools bespeak an absolute simplicity, the plainest forms affording the greatest range of possibilities for the user's hand. That which is overdesigned, too highly specific, anticipates outcome; the anticipation of outcome guarantees, if not failure, the absence of grace.   WILLIAM GIBSON

EXTENDED PRACTICE

SOUNDSPACE ARCHITECTURE FOR SOUND AND VISION

01-03

INTEGRATED DESIGN PROCESSES

Ever since the Renaissance, architects have reduced their activities to a more and more narrowly defined field, to the point of facing obsolescence in many areas of construction. Planning, design and building processes have become increasingly complex and demand more and more collaborative efforts between disciplines. A reluctance to assume responsibility and accountability for the entire project has contributed to marginalizing the architectural profession. Combined practices of architects and structural or building-systems engineers are common in large firms, but generally follow a traditional pattern that is not always easily adaptable to a fast-changing world.

The exploration of alternative practice models is a dominant issue for architects. A team of multidisciplinary experts, working closely together, can deliver a building in a more efficient and predictable manner, while maintaining a central vision and clearly defined goals. A diverse and sophisticated client base demands increased integration and accountability. Alternative approaches such as architect-led design-build contracts and turnkey project delivery, including equipment and furnishings, can offer some answers.

Recent examples have shown architects reclaiming some of the lost territory, and expanding their actions into related fields. Idea-based firms like Rem Koolhaas's OMA are taking advantage of contemporary communications methods and global connections to build networks of international collaborators. No longer limited to designing buildings, they analyze their client's business structures, consult on corporate identities, help develop brands and much more.

Small, specialized fields, such as buildings for media and the arts, are conducive to a tight vertical integration of various disciplines. The related entities directly involved in our projects have developed over time, based on need or demand. The gradual addition of new elements allows the fine-tuning of the collaborative process, an ongoing and open-ended undertaking. Now capable of completing and equipping entire projects , the group is nonetheless open for new developments and additions.

Associations with other, not directly affiliated, groups are equally beneficial, and contribute to a further expansion of services.

the bau:ton group
UMBRELLA ORGANIZATION

---

the bau:ton group.
OVERALL MANAGEMENT

- INTERNAL INFRASTRUCTURE
- INTERNAL BUSINESS SERVICES

- GENERAL ACQUISITIONS
- FACILITATION OF SYNERGIES

- PROJECT MANAGEMENT
- CONSTRUCTION MANAGEMENT

- BUSINESS PLANNING AND CONSULTING
- REAL ESTATE

---

studio **bau:ton**, LLC
ARCHITECTS

- ARCHITECTURE
- STRATEGIC PLANNING

- DESIGN CONCEPTS
- INTERIOR DESIGN

- ACOUSTIC DESIGN

TEC:ton engineering, LLC
TECHNICAL ENGINEERING

- SYSTEMS INTEGRATION
- TECHNICAL PROJECT MANAGEMENT

- EQUIPMENT PACKAGE DESIGN
- EQUIPMENT SALES AND BROKERAGE

- AUDIO/VIDEO EQUIPMENT INSTALLATIONS
- EQUIPMENT WIRING

TEC:ton sound systems
SPECIALTY MANUFACTURING

- LOUDSPEAKER DESIGN AND MANUFACTURE
- ACOUSTIC ELEMENT DESIGN AND MANUFACTURE
- SPECIALTY FURNITURE DESIGN AND MANUFACTURE

LA2f3 constructors, Inc.
GENERAL CONTRACTORS

- GENERAL CONSTRUCTION
- SPECIALTY CONSTRUCTION

- SPECIALTY CONSTRUCTION MANAGEMENT
- SPECIALTY CONSTRUCTION CONSULTING

- SPECIALTY FABRICATIONS
- SPECIALTY INSTALLATIONS

BridgeCo AG
ELECTRONICS AND SOFTWARE DEVELOPMENT

- CONSUMER ELECTRONICS COMMUNICATIONS PLATFORM
- RESEARCH AND DEVELOPMENT

paraDOX acoustics
MANUFACTURING

- LOUDSPEAKER CABINET MANUFACTURE
- ACOUSTIC ELEMENT MANUFACTURE
- FURNITURE MANUFACTURE

artistpro
INFORMATION AND MEDIA RESOURCES

- PUBLISHING AND ADVERTISING
- PUBLISHER OF THE RECORDING INDUSTRY SOURCEBOOK

RipBang Architecture
THEME DESIGN

- RETAIL CONCEPTS
- SPORTS FACILITIES
- BRANDING AND IDENTITIES

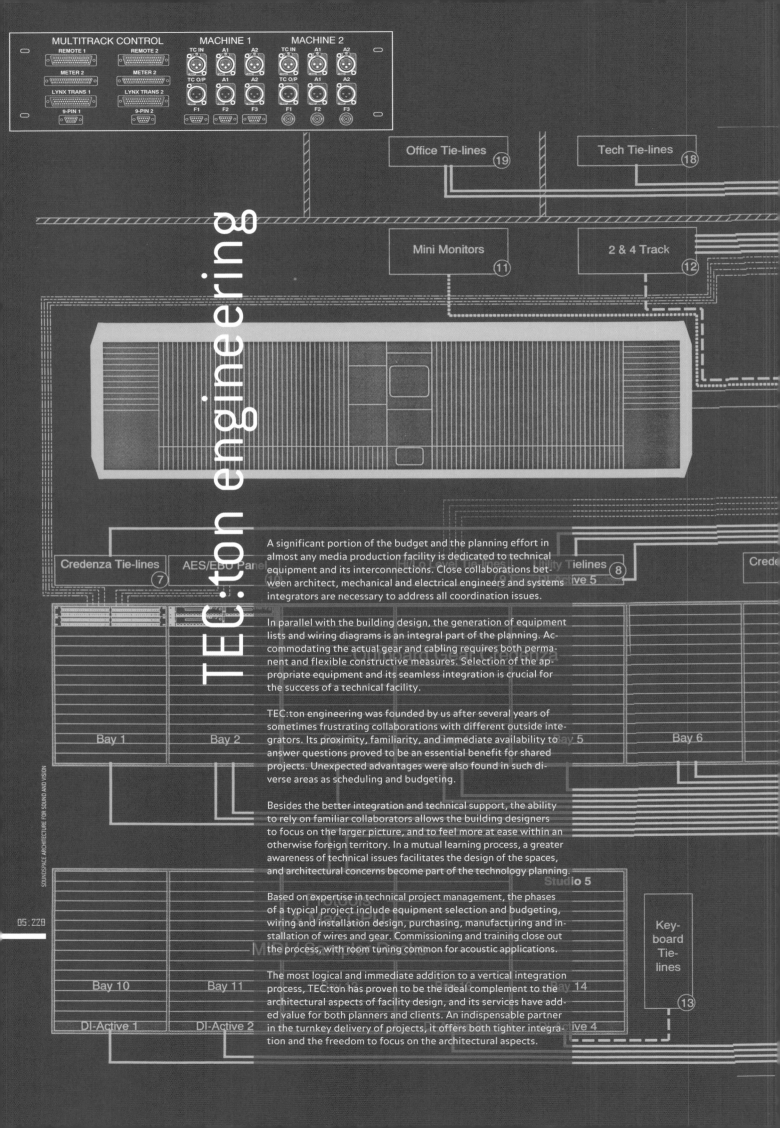

TEC:ton engineering

A significant portion of the budget and the planning effort in almost any media production facility is dedicated to technical equipment and its interconnections. Close collaborations between architect, mechanical and electrical engineers and systems integrators are necessary to address all coordination issues.

In parallel with the building design, the generation of equipment lists and wiring diagrams is an integral part of the planning. Accommodating the actual gear and cabling requires both permanent and flexible constructive measures. Selection of the appropriate equipment and its seamless integration is crucial for the success of a technical facility.

TEC:ton engineering was founded by us after several years of sometimes frustrating collaborations with different outside integrators. Its proximity, familiarity, and immediate availability to answer questions proved to be an essential benefit for shared projects. Unexpected advantages were also found in such diverse areas as scheduling and budgeting.

Besides the better integration and technical support, the ability to rely on familiar collaborators allows the building designers to focus on the larger picture, and to feel more at ease within an otherwise foreign territory. In a mutual learning process, a greater awareness of technical issues facilitates the design of the spaces, and architectural concerns become part of the technology planning.

Based on expertise in technical project management, the phases of a typical project include equipment selection and budgeting, wiring and installation design, purchasing, manufacturing and installation of wires and gear. Commissioning and training close out the process, with room tuning common for acoustic applications.

The most logical and immediate addition to a vertical integration process, TEC:ton has proven to be the ideal complement to the architectural aspects of facility design, and its services have added value for both planners and clients. An indispensable partner in the turnkey delivery of projects, it offers both tighter integration and the freedom to focus on the architectural aspects.

SOUNDSPACE ARCHITECTURE FOR SOUND AND VISION

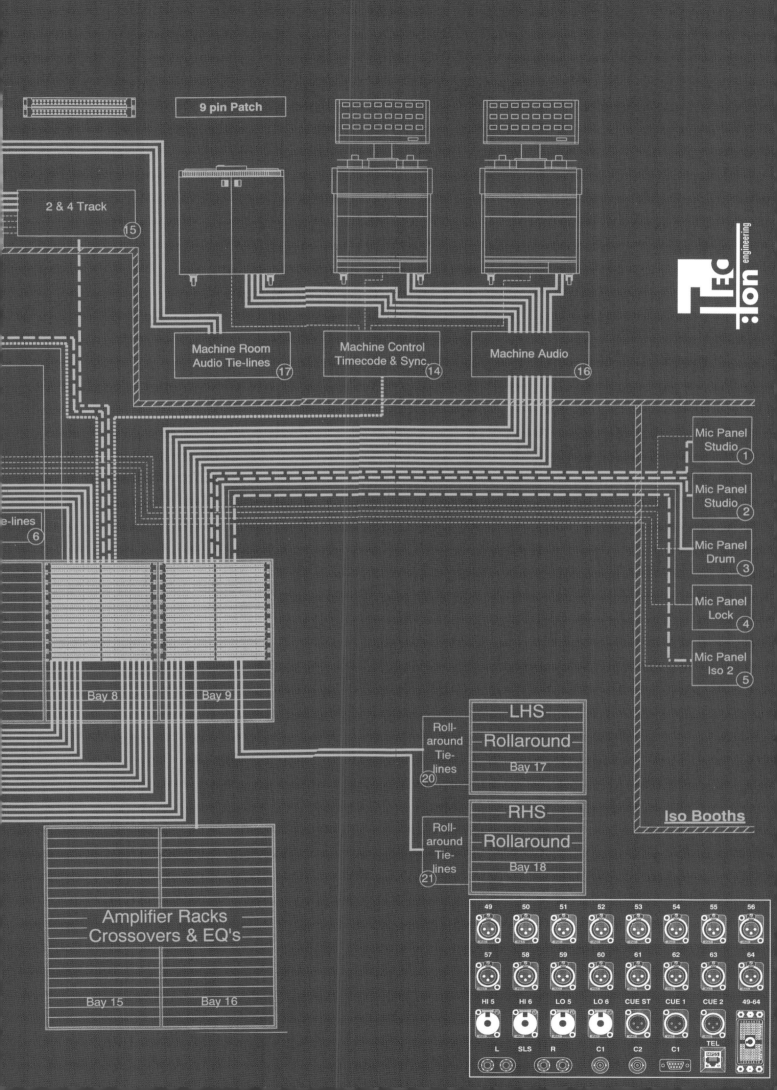

9 pin Patch

2 & 4 Track ⑮

Machine Room
Audio Tie-lines ⑰

Machine Control
Timecode & Sync. ⑭

Machine Audio ⑯

Mic Panel
Studio ①

Mic Panel
Studio ②

Mic Panel
Drum ③

Mic Panel
Lock ④

Mic Panel
Iso 2 ⑤

...e-lines ⑥

Bay 8

Bay 9

Roll-
around
Tie-
lines
⑳

LHS
Rollaround
Bay 17

RHS
Rollaround
Bay 18

Roll-
around
Tie-
lines
㉑

Iso Booths

Amplifier Racks
Crossovers & EQ's

Bay 15

Bay 16

49	50	51	52	53	54	55	56
57	58	59	60	61	62	63	64
HI 5	HI 6	LO 5	LO 6	CUE ST	CUE 1	CUE 2	49-64
L	SLS	R	C1	C2	C1	TEL	

BridgeCo

Designing buildings that try to fully exploit the possibilities of any existing technology can reveal limitations in the status quo. The CitySwitch venture (see page 216) is just one example where the lack of a unified and affordable data-transmissions standard impeded the ultimate goal of providing a continuous entertainment experience for the users.

Christoph Heidelberger, a developer of the first professional analog-to-digital converters for audio applications, and an exceptional authority on microelectronics and broadband technology, was the perfect partner to turn to when confronting these obstacles. Having contemplated the same problems over the years, his discussions with Peter Maurer finally led him to leave a lucrative engineering position and transform his own consulting firm into a new partnership, NET:ton engineering. Once an outstanding team of engineers and business experts had been assembled, BridgeCo AG was founded in Switzerland, along with the studio bau:ton partners and other key members.

With the assistance of KTI, a Swiss semi-governmental agency for the support of promising new technology companies, initial funding was secured. In a very difficult climate for high-tech financing, BridgeCo attracted subsequent rounds of venture capital, and over the following two years was able to raise additional funds that ensured the survival of the company.

Originally based on the premise of developing proprietary network technology for professional audio and video applications, the company adapted its goals when further research showed much greater promise in the consumer market. The fundamental concept of bridging previously independent networks, standards and industries proved adaptable to professional and consumer applications. In early 2003, BridgeCo started rolling out its proprietary microchips, and officially presented the first products by third-party manufacturers incorporating the new technology.

The company's integrated "Entertainment Network Adapter" allows the seamless connection of consumer electronics devices, musical instruments, and personal computers, ultimately creating the long-sought continuum for home entertainment. Beyond bridging the divide between Internet applications and consumer electronics, the company, in view of its roots in the high-end audio and video domains, holds great promise for future expansion into these originally envisioned fields.

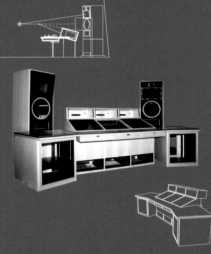

PRODUCT DESIGN

Although building products and audiovisual equipment are generally available in abundance, not all demands can be met with standard off-the-shelf merchandise. Acoustical materials on the market range from the lowly and omnipresent suspended-ceiling tile to sophisticated special devices for controlling sound. Countless manufacturers make electronic equipment, such as loudspeakers, and choices are seemingly endless. But for very specific purposes, or to integrate a material into a particular design, the custom development and manufacturing of certain items is sometimes necessary.

Some manufacturers (such as RPG, for example) offer a wide and meticulously researched line of products, which are often specified and incorporated into our acoustic spaces. Still, in the field of acoustic diffusors we began early on to complement that range of products with our own designs to perfectly suit each application. Collaboration with paraDOX acoustics in Switzerland was the key to developing a line of wood products for use in our own projects.

Fueled by client requests, the proprietary development of loudspeakers for our acoustic designs has also been a part of our ongoing attempts at integration since the early days. Speakers for professional listening are designed and built in collaboration with various component manufacturers and electronic acousticians for individual projects. TEC:ton sound systems offers professional monitors that are specifically tailored to their sonic environment and purpose.

Specialized furniture for workstations needs to be built around the equipment it contains, and, most importantly, it must be ergonomically correct. As an important visual component in a room, its design also needs to be integrated into the overall scheme. Although this is a very individual effort in many cases, certain standardizations have been achieved, and a line of pieces is available as a result of the continual fine-tuning.

Not just limited to technical spaces, the design of furniture and building components is an important part of the overall spatial environment, and can complement and enhance the broader structural architecture.

SOUNDSPACE ARCHITECTURE FOR SOUND AND VISION

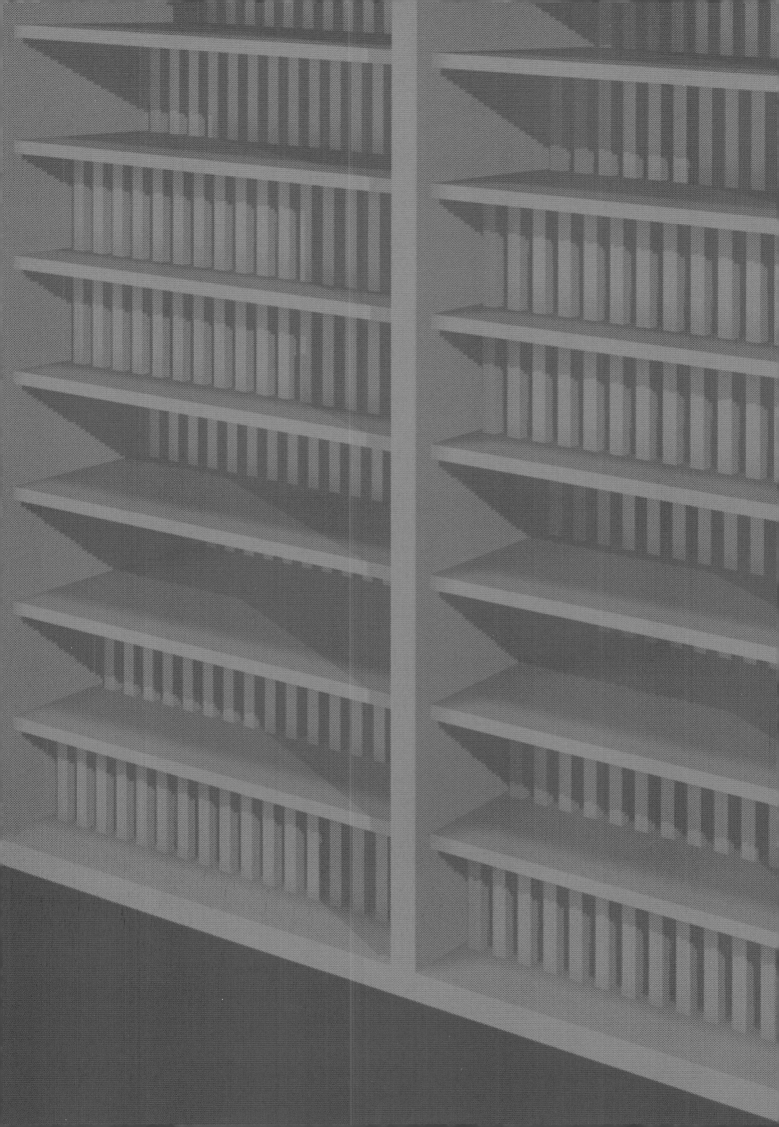

COLLABORATORS / PRINCIPALS

COLLABORATORS

Danielle Arender | Robert Arrand | Banu Ataman
Dan Baroni | Carissa Batiller | Cary Tomas Bellaflor
John Bertram | Stephan Bohne | Jeffrey Bolen | Adele
Bouett | Ross Brennan | Cynthia Bush | Sharon Campbell
Eugene Carpino | Carla Castro | Michael Chung | Jennifer
Connolly | Jason Crowl | Martha Daley | Denton Dance
Martin Danz | Gloria DeLeon | Mark DeMarta | Tino
Dinkoff | Mike Dreher | Laura Finnegan | Eric Fisher
Martha Foley | Meri Freeman | Marta Fuetterer-Fox
Thomas Fuhrer | Bertrand Genoist | Thomas Glauser
Kimberly Grueneisen | Melanie Guralnick | Andreas
Hablutzel | John Hanes | Chris Harrison | David Hecht
Elizabeth Held | Pablo Hermosilla | Graham Hill | Mitja
Hinderks | Ralf Hochstrasser | Ursula Hochstrasser | Insa
Hoffmann | Tom Hoos | Martin Hopitzan | Robert Hsin
Thomas Clayt Hudson | Denise Ip | Charles Irving
Dominik Jenni | David Joho | Lauren Karwoski | Art Kelm
Liza Kerrigan | Ken Kim | Richard Landers | Frank LaTouf
Sue-Meng Lau | Jackie Ledger | Bryan Libit | Michelle
Mee Liu | Jeannie Long | Taylor Louden | Carol Lowry
Pauline Lyders | Briggs MacDonald | Philippe Marmillod
Linda Maze-Chervenak | Jackie McNaney | Doug McNeill
Xochitl Mendez | Esther Meriweather | Ilaria Mazzoleni
Tyler Meyr | Christopher Mueller | Stephan Mundwiler
John Neff | Marni Nelko | George Newburn | Maren Niehoff
Jennifer Ochoa | Justin Patwin | Naina Paul | Tony Pritchard
Andrea Pulch | Anita Putterman | Bernard Reeve | Jim
Rogers | Shawn Rogers | Evan Roth | Duke Sakiyabu | Tricia
Sanedrin | Claris Sayadian | Tanya Scheer | Beat Schenk
Edward Scott | Timothy Shugrue | Shivjit Chevy Sidhu
Timothy Smith | Kimberly Stankey | Charles Swanson
Sid Taylor | Nicola Thomson | Beth Thorne | Isabelle Ulrich
Dominika Waclawiak | Urs Weber | Andy Wild | Troy
Williams | Lisa Spike Wolff | Sherilyn Wolters | Peter
Wowkowych | Ray Yamagata | Lorraine Zecca
Thomas Zürcher | Esther Zumsteg

PETER GRUENEISEN | AIA
Founding Partner
Principal | Architecture
1990 M. Arch., SCI-Arc, Santa Monica
1983 B.Sc. Architectural Engineering Biel, Switzerland

PETER MAURER
Founding Partner
Principal | Business Integration / Synergies
1983 B.Sc. Architectural Engineering Biel, Switzerland

COMPANIES AND INSTITUTIONS

4MC, Singapore | 20th Century Fox, Los Angeles | 525 Post Production, Hollywood
5.1 Entertainment, Santa Monica | American Gramaphone, Omaha | Antara, Vietnam
Artistic Palace, Paris | Audio Resource, Honolulu | Audiobanks, Santa Monica
Anacapa Studio, Malibu | Asymmetrical Productions, Hollywood | Bad Animals, Seattle
Bakery Music, Bangkok | Blue Jay Studio, Hollywood | Brandon's Way, Los Angeles
BridgeCo AG, Zurich | C + C Music, New York | Campus Hollywood, Hollywood
Canyon Charter Elementary School, Los Angeles | Chalice Studios, Hollywood
Century Productions, Las Vegas | Estudios Churubusco Aztecas, Mexico City | Cello
Studios, Hollywood | Center for the Recording Arts, North Hollywood | Cheyenne
Productions, Santa Monica | Cinephase, Paris | CitySwitch, Amsterdam | Club Sugar,
Santa Monica | The Complex, Los Angeles | Counterpoint Studios, Salt Lake City
Creative Cafe, Los Angeles | Crystal Cathedral, Garden Grove | Dajhelon Studios,
Rochester | DARP Studios, Atlanta | Dave Matthews Band, Virginia | Audio Cinema
Duran, Paris | John Debney Productions, Burbank | Def Jam, New York | Digital Domain,
Los Angeles | Disneyland Europe, Paris | Dubeytunes, San Francisco | EFX Systems,
Burbank | Embassy Studios, Weiler | Encore Studios, Burbank | Enterprise Studios,
Burbank | Euphonix, Palo Alto | Experience Music Project, Seattle | Extasy Records,
Los Angeles | Face the Music, New York | FirstLookArt.com, Los Angeles | Fatima,
Bangkok | Freewave Studio, Los Angeles | Future Records, Virginia Beach | Full Sail,
Orlando | The Gordy Company, Hollywood | Gold Coast Studios, Santa Monica
Goodnight LA Studios, Van Nuys | Green Dragon, Amsterdam | Ground Control Studios,
Burbank | Havas Interactive, Los Angeles | In Your Ear, Richmond | International
Recording, Burbank | Internet Holdings Group, Hollywood | Joe's Place, Atlanta | Quincy
Jones Productions, Studio City | Kenter Canyon Elementary School, Brentwood
Klasky/Csupo Inc., Hollywood | Latin World Entertainment, Caracas | LA Contemporary
Dance Theater, Los Angeles | LA Recording Workshop, North Hollywood | LA Studios,
Los Angeles | Lacoco Studios, Atlanta | LaFace Records Inc., Atlanta | Launch
Media, New York/Santa Monica | Leeway Entertainment, Santa Monica | Lime Studios,
Santa Monica | Loomis Productions, Dallas | Margarita Mix, Santa Monica / Hollywood
Matthews/Griffith Music, Hollywood | Maui Island Recorder, Maui | Mega West
Studios, Paris | Mesmer Av Studio, Culver City | Metropol Internet Studio, Los Angeles
Musicians Institute, Hollywood | Musikvergnuegen, Hollywood | National Public
Radio, Culver City | No Limit Records, Baton Rouge | Nova Logic, Calabasas | NRG
Studios, North Hollywood | O'Henry Studios, Burbank | Ocean Way Studios, Nashville
OffPlanet Entertainment, San Francisco | One on One, North Hollywood | Open Films,
Culver City | ORF Studios, Vienna | Our House Inc., Chicago | Post Logic Video,
Hollywood | Power Station, Tokyo | Promise Studio, Taipei | Rap-A-Lot Studios,
Houston | The Record Plant, Hollywood | Rockland Studio, Chicago | Royaltone
Studios, North Hollywood | Rush Media, New York | Howard Schwartz Recording, New
York | Sega Studio, San Francisco | Melisma Records, Atlanta | Signet Sound, West
Hollywood | Sony Music Entertainment (Japan), Tokyo | Studio 56, Hollywood | Studio
Atlantis, Hollywood | Supertracks, Santa Monica | Sure Shot Productions, Alexandria
Swell, Chicago | Sybersound, Malibu | Symphony Studios, Buenos Aires | Syntrax
Studios, Pittsburgh | TAD/Pioneer, Los Angeles | Taisei Corporation, Tokyo | Tate &
Partners, Santa Monica | Tell-a-Vision Post, Hollywood | TF1, Paris | The Track House,
Van Nuys | Thinktank, Chicago | TK Disc America, Honolulu | Tremens Film Tonstudio,
Vienna | Tyrolis Studios, Liechtenstein | University of Alabama, Birmingham | University
of Northern Alabama, Florence | University of Southern California, Los Angeles
USA Network, Hollywood | UTB Television, Hollywood | Virgin Television, Mexico
City | VTU Bach Studio, Vietnam | Villa Muse Studios, Austin | The Walt Disney
Company, Burbank | Westwood One, Culver City | Wilshire Stages, Los Angeles
Wirtschaftskammer Steiermark, Graz | Wonderland Studio, Los Angeles | X-Art
Studios, Pinkafeld | Xtreme New Media, Seattle | Soundproof Studio, Los Feliz
Zona Playa, Santa Monica

INDIVIDUALS

Marc Anthony | Dallas Austin | Jeff Ayeroff and Marty Longbine | Michael Bay | Carter
Beauford | Christophe Beck | Walter Becker | Pat Benatar and Neil Ghiraldo | Brian
Bennett | Bruce and Marie Botnick | David and Sarah Bottjer | Bill Bottrell | William
Brewer | Bobby Brown | Tracy Chapman | Ben Cole | Stewart Copeland | Bob Crewe
Mike D | Erin Davis | Ben Decter | Paul DeMyer | Ian Dye | Kenneth "Babyface" Edmonds
Steve Edwards | Jeff Fair and Star Parodi | Perry Farrell | Gregg Field and Monica
Mancini | Peter Frampton | Brendan Fraser | Curtis Freilich | John Frizzell | Parmer Fuller
Barry Gibb | Brian Austin Green | Jim and Patty Greenwood | Joel and Murielle
Hamilton | Craig Harris | Tom Hormel | James Newton Howard | Ice-T | Delight Jenkins
Jirasupakorn Family | R Kelly | Tetsuya Komuro | James and Ron Last | Rhett Lawrence
Howard and Alisa Levine | Dana Levy and Tish O'Connor | James Linahon | David Lynch
Master P | Dieter Meier | LeRoi Moore | Jon Newkirk | David Newman | Wayne and
Noriko Peet | Bonnie Raitt | Paul Reynolds | Teddy Riley | Barry Rose | David and
Michelle Sack | Philippe Sarde | Kimi Sato | Ben Schultz | Michael and Donna Sedgwick
Silkk the Shocker | Will Smith | Rick Stevens | Robin Thicke | Rose Van Dyke | David
Vogel | Joss Whedon | Patrick Williams | Robert and Jan Williford | Richard and Wendy
Windebank | Peter Wolf | David Wolper | Stevie Wonder

CREDITS

PHOTOGRAPHS AND ILLUSTRATIONS	PICTURE NUMBERS
Robert Alexander	02:022:01; 02:023:02
Michael Brewster	02:026:01/ 02
BridgeCo AG	05:230:01/ 02/ 03
Archiv Susanne Schindler	02:023:03/ 04
Jim Bourg/ Reuters	02:029:05
Andreas Bruckner	04:099:04/ 05; 04:101:02
City of Los Angeles	04:105:02
Edward Colver	04:104:01; 04:109:01/ 02/ 03; 04:145:03; 04:172: 01/ 02/ 03; 04:173: 04/ 05; 04:175:01; 04:176:01/ 02/ 03/ 04; 04:190:01/ 02; 04:191:03; 04:202:01/ 02; 04:209:01/ 04
Jim Crowley	02:028:01
Peter D'Antonio, RPG Diffusor Systems	03:065:31/ 33
Bengt-Inge Dalenbäck, CATT-Acoustic	03:065:32
Stephan Doleschal	04:098:01/ 02/ 03; 04:099:06; 04:100:01
John Ellis	01:015:05; 01:016:02
Thomas Flechtner	02:030:01; 02:031:02; 02:033:06
Sir Banister Fletcher, *A History of Architecture* edited by John Musgrove	03:059:09
David Franzen	04:154:01; 04:155:02; 04:157:01/ 02/ 03/ 04/ 05/ 06/ 07; 04:160:01/ 02/ 03/ 04
Denis Freppel	01:015:07; 04:140:01/ 02; 04:141:03; 04:142:01/ 02; 04:143:03; 04:145:01/ 02; 04:147:01; 04:179:02/ 03/ 04; 04:183:01/ 03/ 04/ 05; 04:184:01/ 02/ 03
House-Ear-Institute, Los Angeles	03:053:05
Luc Hautecoeur	04:103:01/ 02/ 03
Bob Hodas	02:038:01/ 02/ 03/ 04; 02:039:05/ 06/ 07
Sachiko Kodama, Minako Takeno	02:020:01; 02:021:02
Toby Keeler	04:178:01
Kazumi Kurigami / Camel	04:132:02; 04:133:05/ 06/ 07/ 08; 04:137:01
Brandon LaBelle	02:025:03/ 04; 02:027:03
Ron Lagerlof	04:211:01/ 02/ 03
Lawrence Manning / Corbis	04:206:01
Thomas McIntosh, Emmanuel Madan	02:034:02; 02:035:03; 02:036:02
Walter Meir	02:031:03; 02:032:01; 02:033:07
John Neff	04:183:02
Obayashi Corporation	04:132:01/ 03; 04:133:04/ 09; 04:134:01/ 02
Daniel Ott	02:032:02/ 03/ 04/ 05
Norio Ozaki / Camel	04:131:01
Philips Company Archives	02:024:01/ 02
Grant Ramaly	04:091:01/ 02/ 03; 04:092:01/ 02; 04:093:03/ 04/ 05
RipBang / studio bau:ton	05:224:01/ 02/ 03
Philippe Ruault	03:064:27
Frédéric Ste-Marie	02:037:03
Diana Shearwood	02:034:01; 02:035:04; 02:036:01; 02:037:04
J. Scott Smith	04:110:01/ 02; 04:112:01/ 02/ 03/ 04; 04:113:05; 04:115:01/ 02/ 03/ 04; 04:187:01/ 02; 04:189:01/ 02
Tapio Takala and The Digital Virtual Acoustics Group	03:065:30
Jeff Talman / Bitforms	02:041:01/ 02/ 03
Underwood & Underwood / Corbis	04:166:01
Joshua White	04:094:01/ 02/ 03/ 04; 04:095:05/ 06/ 07; 04:097:01/ 02; 04:169:01; 04:170:01/ 02/ 03; 04:171:04/ 05; 04:211:07/ 08
Joshua White / Frank O. Gehry & Partners	03:065:29
James Wilson	04:152:01; 04:153:02
Scot Zimmerman	04:116:01/ 02/ 03; 04:117:04/ 05
Gerald Zugmann	02:029:02/ 03

All other photographs and illustrations © studio bau:ton

Every effort was made to acknowledge and obtain permission for all pictures.
We deeply regret any mistakes or oversights that might have occurred.

ORIGINAL PUBLICATIONS

Peter Zumthor with Plinio Bachmann, Karoline Gruber, Ida Gut, Daniel Ott,
Max Rigendinger, edited by Roderick Hönig, *Swiss Sound Box:
A Handbook for the Pavilion of the Swiss Confederation at Expo 2000 in
Hanover*, Birkhäuser, Basel / Boston / Berlin 2000

Wolf D. Prix / Coop Himmern(l)au, *Maximum Directness*.
First published in: *Im Profil* 30, 24 July 1995

Thomas McIntosh, Emanuell Madan, *Silophone*.
Parts of the essay have been published in:
Espace magazine, www.espace-sculpture.com, December 2001

TRANSLATIONS AND SOURCES FOR QUOTES

ENDPAPER FRONT

Hans Scharoun, *Essay to the opening of the Philharmonic Hall, Berlin*.
In: *Philharmonic Hall Berlin*, Leaflet to the opening on 10.15.1963
Berliner Philharmonisches Orchester, Thorman & Goetsch, Berlin

ENDPAPER BACK

Daniel Libeskind, *The Walls are Alive*. Guardian Unlimited,
Guardian Newspapers Limited, London 07.13.2002

PAGE 6

Wilhelm Joseph von Schelling, *Philosophie der Kunst*.
Wiss. Buchgesellschaft, Darmstadt 1976
(...) architecture in general is frozen music.

PAGE 7

Anne Louise Germaine de Staël-Holstein,
Courinne ou l'Italie. Garnier, Paris 1880
*The sight of such a monument is like continual and stationary music
which one hears for one's good as one approaches it.*

PAGE 7

Johann Wolfgang von Goethe, *Letter to Eckermann*, 03.23.1829.
In: Johann Peter Eckermann, *Gespräche mit Goethe in den letzten
Jahren seines Lebens*. Dt. Klassiker Verlag, Frankfurt 1999

PAGE 8

Steen Eiler Rasmussen, *Experiencing Architecture*.
The M.I.T Press, Cambridge 1962

PAGE 18

Edward O. Wilson, *Consilience: The Unity of Knowledge*.
A Borzoi Book, Alfred A.Knopf Inc., New York 1998

PAGE 42

Vitruvius, *Ten Books on Architecture*. Translation by Ingrid D. Rowland,
Cambridge University Press, Cambridge 1999
"Reprinted with the permission of Cambridge University Press"

PAGE 72

Mstislav Rostropovich, *The Right Place*. J.S.Bach, Cello Suiten,
EMI Classica, Booklet, EMI records, Ltd. 1995

PAGE 86

Joe Jackson, *Body and Soul*. AM Records, AMLX 65000, Liner Notes 1984

PAGE 194

Paul D. Lehrman, *Mix, The Right Stuff*.
Music and Technology at the Hartt School. November 2002

PAGE 206

Björk, *Wired Magazine* 10.05, *Beat Manifestos*. May 2002

PAGE 214

Cary Sherman in: Josef Proegler, *Mapping the Musical Commons:
Digitization, Simulation, Speculation*. www. firstmonday.dk, Internet Journal

PAGE 222

William Gibson, *All Tomorrow's Parties*. G.P.Putnam's Sons, New York 1999

As an architect and as someone who studied and performed music, I have been keenly aware of the intense and often reciprocal dialogue between the audible and the visible. Buildings provide spaces for living, but are also de facto instruments, giving shape to the sound of the world. Music and architecture are related not only by metaphor, but also through concrete space. Every building I have admired is, in effect, a musical instrument whose performance gives space a quality that often seems to be transcendent and immaterial. The ineffable or the immeasurable gives a sense of wonder that forms the difference between building and architecture. Perception and measurement link music and architecture through the tradition of composition in both arts. The idea of harmony, discovered by the Pythagoreans in ancient Greece, describes the mystery in which the length of vibrating strings corresponds to golden section proportions in space. However, it is not only this aspect that connects space with the idea of cosmic order. There is an even deeper connection between the genesis of architecture in a drawing and the composition of music on the five-line staff and its transformation into a public performance. Musical compositions performed through the large forces of an orchestra and architectural drawings used as a means to transmit form into civic space are more than analogous — they are the constructive realities in both arts. The dimension of time shared by both architecture and music provides a critical difference and a critical connection between them. Since music is experienced in time, its impact is related to the unique silence that follows, giving the musical work a memorable and dynamic stability. In architecture, however, the static nature of constructed space gains a dimension of perspective through experience and anticipation. Architecture can only be appreciated by transforming size into scale, matter into light, and time into rhythm,